What Teachers, Administrators, and Trade Authors Say About *Disrupting Thinking*

If you're ready to understand that children are more than test scores; if you're ready to take a hard look at hard topics; if you're ready to have your own thinking disrupted, challenged, questioned; if you are really ready to teach all children and give them equitable instruction, then *Disrupting Thinking* is the book for you.

—**TONYA PERRY, Ph.D., Assistant Professor of Secondary Education, University of Alabama at Birmingham, Co-Director UAB Red Mountain Writing Project**

Kylene Beers and Bob Probst have done it again. They have given us exactly what we need precisely when we need it. *Disrupting Thinking* shows us how to challenge the mindset that students use when reading to strengthen critical understandings that lead to the deepest learning.

—**MORGAN DUNTON, English Language Arts Specialist, Maine Department of Education**

This book is a reminder that we are not in the business of raising readers who can merely retell a story or pass a test. Instead we are growing responsive, responsible, empathic readers who come away from a text with a better understanding of other people, their world, and themselves.

—**FRANKI SIBBERSON, National Council of Teachers of English 2017 Vice President, 3rd grade teacher, author of *Still Learning to Read***

Educators who understand the power and influence of literacy know the depth of the work of Beers and Probst. They stand on the front line working to capture, inspire, and teach a new generation of learners. As a superintendent, I constantly search for the best resources to facilitate academic advancement. *Disrupting Thinking* is a resource we can't wait to get our hands on!

—**STEPHEN G. PETERS, Ed.D., Superintendent, Laurens County School District 55**

Those of us who love words and understand the power of words can rejoice! *Disrupting Thinking* is the book educators, parents, and our democracy need. Read it to find the motivation and the vital tools required to create a generation of readers whose robust literacy skills and enthusiasm for reading will help them grow and change the world.

—**LAURIE HALSE ANDERSON, National Book Award Finalist, author of many books including *The Impossible Knife of Memories*, *Speak*, and *Ashes***

In their inimitable style, Kylene and Bob urge us to ask, "How has this text changed me?" At this moment, this is the most important point for all of us because "...our democracy is best served when we encourage students to begin at an early age to pay close attention both to what the text says and to what they feel and think as they read. Not one or the other, but both."

—**LESTER L. LAMINACK, Consultant and Author of *The Ultimate Read-Aloud Resource* and *Best Friend Fiction Collection***

If you want to motivate students to become responsive, responsible, and compassionate readers; if you want to move students beyond finding evidence to answer questions to generating their own questions; if you want your students to read with the goal of becoming better people, then you must read this timely and timeless book.

—**MICHELLE MILLER, 3rd grade teacher, Solon City Schools, Solon, OH**

With so many things competing for our students' attention, reading often finishes in last place. And when kids do read in school, it is often a lifeless exercise geared toward passing the test. Beers and Probst aim to change all of that. They offer teachers a wise and practical framework that will show our readers the power, joy, and importance of becoming lifelong readers.

—**GAIL BOUSHEY & JOAN MOSER, "The 2 Sisters," webmasters of the2sisters.com, authors of *The Daily 5* and *The CAFÉ Book***

The beauty of this book is that in advocating for purposeful instruction that helps students become responsive, responsible, compassionate readers, it creates a vision for how teachers can help students change the world.

—JAN BURKINS & KIM YARIS, authors of *Who's Doing the Work: How to Say Less So Readers Can Do More*

This is THE book we need most right now as we challenge our students to become purposeful readers who question and challenge texts. It is a rallying cry that reminds us that teaching is about so much more than raising test scores. Beers and Probst explain relevance in a way that changes everything I will do tomorrow.

—SARA KAJDER, Ph.D., author of *Adolescents and Digital Literacies* and *Bringing the Outside In: Visual Ways to Engage Reluctant Readers*

As always, when I read Kylene and Bob's words, I'm already nodding and nodding and nodding— 'til my neck starts hurting. How is it that they always ask just the right questions and pinpoint what needs to be addressed so exactly?

—ALLISON JACKSON, 3rd grade teacher, Waggoner Elementary School, Tempe, AZ

A timely and critically important must-read for all who care about our children's future as informed, engaged, and compassionate citizens. This book reaches deeply into our hearts and minds as it disrupts our thinking about what the power of reading really means and where it begins—in our classrooms.

—GAIL WESTBROOK, Elementary Literacy Specialist, Evergreen Public Schools, Vancouver, WA

Kylene and Bob brilliantly explain the tragedy of disconnected reading, where students only read to complete a task, thereby trampling the joy of chasing after a story or an idea. They explain what educators can do to disrupt this trend, encourage classroom talk, and nurture lifelong readers, who in turn will make up an informed citizenry.

—SARA HOLBROOK, Poet and Educator, Author of *Practical Poetry* and *High-Impact Writing Clinics* with co-author Michael Salinger

Beers and Probst tackle one of teachers' greatest challenges: student apathy. They show us not only how to "teach struggling readers, but how to teach readers to struggle." And then they go the next step and show us how to turn the apathetic reader into a lifetime reader. And for both, we are grateful.

—DANNY BRASSELL, Ph.D., consultant and author of *The Lazy Readers' Book Club*

We're living in a world in which social media and fake news have the potential to shape who we are and what we believe. Through the strategies presented in *Disrupting Thinking*, teachers see clearly how to help students become active participants in constructing meaning, as they respond, question, and challenge, so that in the end they become more responsible citizens in our world.

—MINDY HOFFAR, All Write Consortium Director

Disrupting Thinking is one of the best books I've read about the power of books to disrupt complacency and promote change and the role teachers play in that disruption. Skillfully, these authors address the continuum of education K–12, making this book ideal for colleagues to read and share horizontally and vertically across grade levels.

—SARAH MULHERN GROSS, English teacher at High Technology High School, contributor to *The NY Times* Learning Network

KYLENE BEERS & ROBERT E. PROBST

DISRUPTING THINKING

Why *How* We Read Matters

Photos ©: cover: Henrik Sorensen/Getty Images; back cover: Jeff Williams; 10 and classroom photos throughout: Ken Blaze; 40: Jake Naughton; 63 and teacher charts and student work throughout: Eileen Ours, Linda Rief, Alison Aten, Megan Clappin, and Heidi Weber; 64: Nik01ay/iStockphoto; 74 Kylene Beers headshot and throughout: Lester L. Laminack; 74 Robert E. Probst headshot and throughout: Kylene Beers; 100: katkov/iStockphoto; 103 megaphone: vasabii/iStockphoto; 103 books: ShowVectorStudio/iStockphoto; 103 silhouette with speech balloons: VLADGRIN/iStockphoto; 103 maze: Nik01ay/iStockphoto; 106: Fedorov Oleksiy/Shutterstock, Inc.; 108: michaelquirk/iStockphoto; 114: Bet_Noire/iStockphoto; 134 handshake heart icon: chege011/iStockphoto; 134 fingerprint: tkacchuk/iStockphoto; 134 all other icons: vasabii/iStockphoto; 136 clock: Im-kseniabond/iStockphoto; 136 books: Kittisak_Taramas/iStockphoto; 139: Robert E. Probst.

Screenshot from LittleMissMatched.com copyright © 2017 by LittleMissMatched. Used by permission of LittleMissMatched.

Excerpts from *Scholastic Kids & Family Reading Report*, 5th edition copyright © 2015 by Scholastic Inc. Published by Scholastic Inc.

"The Journey" from *Dream Work* by Mary Oliver. Copyright © 1986 by Mary Oliver. Used by permission of Atlantic Monthly Press.

"Differences in Print Exposure" graphic from "Educator's Briefing, March 2008" copyright © 2008 by Scientific Learning Corporation. Used by permission of Scientific Learning Corporation.

All rights reserved.

Publisher/Acquiring Editor: Lois Bridges
Development Editor: Raymond Coutu
Production Editor: Danny Miller
Editorial Director/Video Editor: Sarah Longhi
Cover designer: Brian LaRossa
Interior designer: Maria Lilja

Scholastic is constantly working to lessen the environmental impact of our manufacturing processes. To view our industry-leading paper procurement policy, visit www.scholastic.com/paperpolicy.

2 3 4 5 6 7 8 9 10 11   40   26 25 24 23 22 21 20 19 18 17

♻ Text pages printed on 10% PCW recycled paper.

CONTENTS

WHERE THE STORY BEGINS

IT WAS A CHILD, a child wearing mismatched socks, who started us thinking about disruptions. She was young—maybe seven or eight years old—and she was happily skipping down the school hallway. While her smile was broad, it was her brightly colored, totally mismatched socks that caught our attention. She stopped in front of us.

Student: Are you visiting my school?

Bob: We are!

Student: Do you like my socks?

Kylene: I do!

Student: Did you notice they don't match? But that's okay, because socks don't actually have to match, you know. There's no rule or anything.

And then she was gone. She continued her dance down the hall, leaving us convinced that, indeed, socks don't have to match. We talked about her with a teacher who said that the sock company LittleMissMatched was the thing in their school. We hadn't heard of it, but now, looking back, we wonder if it didn't plant the seed for the idea that became this book.

Understanding Disruptions

LittleMissMatched launched as a company in 2004 after its founders, Jason Dorf, Arielle Eckstut, and Jonah Staw, all laughed about how socks always disappear in the dryer. They thought it would be better to do two things: sell socks in threes and sell them as zany mismatched designs.

This wacky (and yet successful) idea grew out of two radical thoughts. First, the founders wanted to disrupt the frustration of being stuck with that one lone sock when the other disappeared wherever it is they disappear to in the dryer. Second, they wanted to disrupt the assumption that socks need to match. Where did that idea

Read about this dynamic company at http://littlemiss matched.com/about-us.

originate and why has it been followed for so long? Eventually, they launched their online store to sell socks in packs of three, and now they offer girls "who share our passion for showing our creativity and self-expression" many items in addition to socks.

When disruptions occur, we rarely know just where they will end. Whoever thought that figuring out a way for computers to talk to one another would eventually lead to the Internet, which would eventually lead to the demise of nearly all travel agencies as Expedia, Hotels.com, and other travel sites took their place? Disruptions start with a thought that something needs to be better. And with two questions:

1. What needs to change?
2. What assumptions make that change hard?

And while answering those questions, we need to be willing to

- Be brave. You aren't thinking outside the box. You're hunting for a new one.

- Accept failure. Whatever you're going to do probably won't work the first time or the fifteenth.

- Be open. Disruptions can't proceed in secret. Tell folks what you're trying. Document. Put it up online. Be transparent.

- Be connected. Look around and see who else is trying something similar. Reach out. Talk. Share.

- Get uncomfortable. Disruptions ought to shake us up as we head into uncharted territory. That's okay.

Kylene: Years ago, I asked Bob if he wanted to write an article with me about teaching struggling readers. He said yes, but added he wanted to title it "Teaching Struggling Readers; Teaching Readers to Struggle." While we never wrote the article, we always remembered that title. It captured a shift in our thinking that has guided much of our work. We do believe that unless we all learn how to struggle through a text when the text is tough, we will not be prepared for all the tough texts each of us will undoubtedly face from time to time. Some texts are tough because we lack enough prior knowledge; others are tough because the vocabulary is technical or obscure; many are tough because the ideas are abstract or the syntax is complex. Some are tough because of the images they share, images of war and pain, of loss and hurt, of hunger and loneliness. Of fear.

You somehow shut out the loud voices that proclaim our schools are failing and keep true to the voices that you know matter most: your students' voices.

And some texts are tough because they require us to consider tough issues: our political biases; our racial prejudices; our religious convictions. They are tough because they ask us to read about the shooting of school children; the bombing of marathon spectators; the homeless; the suicide of another fourteen-year-old who has been bullied relentlessly; the slaughter of those in a movie theater or a gay nightclub.

Those are truly tough texts.

Not long after the events of 9/11, Bob wrote an article titled, "Difficult Days, Difficult Texts" for *Voices from the Middle*. In it, he talks about our response to that most difficult of days and our (in)ability to understand the events as they unfolded. He wrote that our students won't learn how to read these difficult texts by

> "...taking quizzes or preparing for them, or by collecting points and prizes for numbers of books read, but by engaging stories and poems that touch them, reading them in the company of other students and committed teachers who will help them make connections, explore responses, raise and answer questions.... Without those stories, and without the ability to read them responsively and responsibly, feeling at least some of the pain and the loss, our students will remain separate, distant, unconnected, vulnerable. If we learn to read them, we may learn to watch the news of difficult days and think responsibly about what we see and hear and be better able to read not only the texts, but our very lives" (2001, p. 53).

If this reader, this student who must be able to handle the toughest of texts, has a chance to emerge in our classrooms, it will be because of teachers who, at the end of a long day, still pause to pick up a professional book and contemplate new ideas. It will be because you watch each child walk through your classroom doors and see our hope for tomorrow. It will be because you somehow shut out the loud voices that proclaim our schools are failing and keep true to the voices that you know matter most: your students' voices.

As writers, the voices we heard loudest were yours. We have listened to your questions, your concerns, your excitement, your joys, and your frustrations. As part of the research for this book, we asked teachers to identify major impediments to the deep learning we all want for students. Repeatedly, a common answer was "apathy." As we've explored this with you, one teacher said, "It's as if they are in a stupor, somehow just going through the motions, even getting good grades, but nothing is really sinking in."

Perhaps it was that comment more than any other that encouraged us to begin talking more generally with hundreds of you across the country. As we visited schools and ran workshops, we asked teachers and teacher leaders about what change was most needed. Repeatedly, the word "thinking" emerged in conversations. Changing how kids think seemed to be on everyone's mind.

And so, *Disrupting Thinking* is, at its heart, an exploration of how we help students become the reader who does so much more than decode, recall, or choose the correct answer from a multiple-choice list. This reader is responsive, aware of her feelings and thoughts as the text brings them forth. She is responsible, reflecting honestly about what the writer has offered and how she has reacted, willing either to hold fast or to change, as reason and evidence dictate. And she is compassionate, willing to imagine, possibly to feel, always to think about what others—

author, characters, and other readers—are experiencing and saying so that she may better understand. Such a reader comes to the text with a determination to learn, and with a desire for the change, slight or dramatic, that learning will bring about. This is a reader who allows her thinking to be disrupted, altered, changed.

The children shown throughout this book are students from the Solon Public Schools, Solon, Ohio. We appreciate the teachers who invited us into their classrooms and the children who were willing to let us work with them.

We hope that this book disrupts your thinking, too. We hope it spurs conversation that you have first with yourself and then with us as you jot notes in the margins of the book, join us at workshops, or connect with us via social media. We encourage you to have conversations with your colleagues about the ideas presented here. And, most important, we hope this book invites conversations with your students. We believe teachers change tomorrow for their students. We're excited to share our thinking with you, today. It's a scary thing—to put a book into a reader's hands. We never know what you, that reader, will do with it. We don't know how it will change you, if it will change you. But now it's yours, and it is you who will give it meaning. We put the words on the page; you bring them to life. And so, together, we turn the page.

Take Two: Introduction

Throughout the book, you'll see "Take Two" video clips of us discussing a point so we can extend the conversation. Go to scholastic.com/BeersandProbst to join us now as we discuss how this book came to be.

PART I
THE READERS WE WANT

Opening Comments

WE'RE OFTEN ASKED where we get our ideas for books. While one of us might quickly say "over a glass of wine," the other would point out that's *when* we get our ideas. The *where* is much more likely to come from classrooms, as we talk with students and teachers or see children wearing mismatched socks. That's exactly where this book began. Take a look at some of the conversations we've had with students recently.

A first grader

Kylene: Why do you think your teacher is teaching you to read?

Jason: Because the whole world can read!

Kylene: Do you have a favorite book?

Jason: *This Book Has No Pictures*. I LOVE that book. It is so so so so so so so so funny.

A third grader

Bob: Why do you think your teacher is teaching you to read?

Rachel: You HAVE to learn to read so you can READ!

Bob: Do you have a favorite book?

Rachel: I LOVE *Bunnicula*. But it's a home book. First my mom read it to me every night. I can't read it at school because I'm not that level. I have to read *Frog and Toad* at school because that's my level. But I LOVE *Bunnicula*. Have you read it? It is soooo funny.

A fourth grader

Bob: Why do you think your teacher is teaching you to read?

Curt: I already can read. Now we just work on *can you find the evidence*.

Bob: Evidence for what?

Curt: I don't know. Like when the teacher asks you a question then you have to find the evidence.

Bob: Do you like to read?

Curt: I did when I was little. Now it is about "Do you know your reading level?" and "Can you show me the evidence?" Sometimes on Fridays we get to just read and then you just read and read and you even forget you are reading. But that's only on the Fridays when no one has a red mark by their name on the behavior chart.

A seventh grader

Kylene: Do your teachers give you reading assignments?

Monica: Sometimes. If we have a story, like in ELA, but, no, not too much.

Kylene: Do you like to read?

Monica: What do you mean?

Kylene: Well, I just wonder if you enjoy reading.

Monica: I like it when Ms. Cox reads us books. She does that and I like that a lot. Right now she's reading us *The Wednesday Wars*. I like that one a lot.

Kylene: Do you read on your own?

Monica: Like for homework?

Kylene: For homework and for fun.

Monica: For fun? Fun? I don't think so.

An eighth grader

Bob: Why do you think your teacher talks about improving reading skills?

Logan: I have absolutely no idea.

Bob: No idea?

Logan: Well, maybe so our Lexile goes up and we can pass the test.

Take Two

Go to scholastic.com/ BeersandProbst to view a conversation between us as we describe the research methods used for this book.

A freshman in college

Kylene: How is reading in your college classes different from the reading you did your last couple of years in high school?

John: Well, first, there is a lot and I mean *a lot* more reading now. Second, in high school, in your textbook, it just told you what was important. Highlighted in yellow for you. And another thing, in high school, in science or social studies, the teachers had a lot of PowerPoints and all you had to do was copy them down. Some teachers didn't assign any reading. In my classes now, the professors begin by asking you to explain what was the most important part of what you read. You can't skip reading and the book isn't going to tell you. You have to figure out on your own what's important to you.

As we looked at the comments made by these students from first grader to college freshman, we saw students move from reading for pure enjoyment to reading to reach a certain Lexile or to pass a test. Reading at a certain level, reading to find evidence, reading to pass a test—all those issues seemed to crowd out any personal reasons for reading. Our youngest students begin school eager to become friends with *Baby Mouse*, *George and Martha*, and *Dory Fantasamagory*, and far too many of our graduating seniors leave having mastered the art of fake reading. Then, if they head to college as did John, the amount of reading can be overwhelming.

> Fake readers pretend to read the text, feign engagement, and sometimes extract words from the text to answer questions with little thought.

We've been thinking about this issue—this turn away from reading—for much of our professional lives. We have studied and written about students, texts, and teachers. We've written about helping underachieving readers and reluctant readers. We've wondered if the problem of aliteracy could be solved by giving kids books they wanted to read and making sure they had more time to read. And for decades many teachers have tried doing just that. We know that during a student's experiences in kindergarten through high school, perhaps more so in those elementary years, many teachers encourage a love of reading; yet the overwhelming majority of our high school students do not identify themselves as readers and do not turn to reading for enjoyment (see Chart A). Too often, the right book created a compliant one-book-at-a-time reader, that kid who will willingly read the book we promise him he will enjoy. And yet, he doesn't become the committed reader who searches on his own for the next great book.

And then we wondered if we were trying to solve the wrong problem. Many teachers have given them the right books to read, and many have given them time to read. Perhaps what was missing was helping students have the right mindset while reading. Once we reframed the problem, we began to understand why *how* kids read matters so very much.

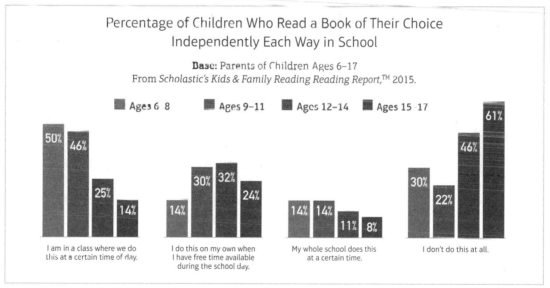

Percentage of Children Who Read a Book of Their Choice Independently Each Way in School

Base: Parents of Children Ages 6–17
From *Scholastic's Kids & Family Reading Reading Report,*™ 2015.

Ages 6–8 ■ Ages 9–11 ■ Ages 12–14 ■ Ages 15–17

- I am in a class where we do this at a certain time of day. — 50%, 46%, 25%, 14%
- I do this on my own when I have free time available during the school day. — 14%, 30%, 32%, 24%
- My whole school does this at a certain time. — 14%, 14%, 11%, 8%
- I don't do this at all. — 30%, 22%, 46%, 61%

CHART A

Chapter 1

Tomorrow's Leaders

IN 2008, Marcus was fourteen years old and in eighth grade. He lived with his mom and younger sister, Jasmine, in a well-kept three-room apartment. His mom and sister shared a bed in the one bedroom while Marcus slept on the couch.

It was easy to see that Marcus adored his sister and watched after her as they walked to the bus stop each morning. His mom was adamant that her two children would be in school each day with homework done, and done neatly. While Marcus quickly describes how well Jasmine is doing in school, he's more guarded when talking about his own progress:

> "I'm not, not so good in school, you know? I don't like it. [pause] My teacher, she's real nice and everything. But, it's just like nothing we do there is going to change anything here."

Marcus is referring to the landscape of his neighborhood, a landscape that suggests parents who work hard just to put food on the table. He continued: "This is my world. How's the word-of-the-day help with this?"

Though Marcus seems to simply move through the routine of the school day with little interest, he turns, as often as he can, to a spiral notebook he keeps close. When asked what he's writing, he replies that "it's kinda private" and explains that the writing he does in the notebook is the "wrong kinda writing for school." He says that it doesn't have topic sentences: "This is just my thinking. Like at school, you need topic sentences." When asked if he likes to write, he took a moment to answer and then said,

> "No I don't think so. [pause] I got a D in writing last year. I turned in this one paper about the time my dad came

Bob: Kylene first wrote about Marcus in "The Sounds of Silence," which you can read at scholastic.com/BeersandProbst.

for a visit and the teacher says it was good but it had
agreement errors and that was why it had to get a D.
[pause] I thought it was better than a D. Like maybe a B."

Marcus went on to explain, "What I say don't matter. It's just all
about is it on the rubric and is it agreement and is it correct. It's not ever
about what you really are saying. Write stupid and get a good grade."

Marcus's paper might have had errors, but his voice is clear and his
message profound:

*My Dad's ball swishes through the net like he swishes through
my life. Barely touching anything. But counting all the same.*

Why discuss Marcus and his writing in a book about reading?
Two reasons: first, Marcus is one of those kids you never forget. We carry
his story with us and wanted it in this book. He is most certainly one
of those kids who disrupted our own thinking about school. Second,
Marcus said something about writing that we have heard other kids
say time and time again about reading: "What I say don't matter."
When a right answer is most important, students come to believe their
thoughts don't matter.

Too often we've heard students tell us that they "hate reading"
because it is "dumb," "stupid," and "boring." When we push them to
tell us why, we must admit the most common first response is "I don't
know," which is followed by "It just is." But if we're patient, we'll usually
get more:

- "Because the stories, they are just dumb."

- "It's read and then answer questions and read and then answer
  questions."

- "We had to read *Hatchet* and it was a good book and everything
  but then it was like *stupid* [stress added by student] with all these
  vocabulary and Venn diagrams to make. Stupid."

- "We always have these questions to answer. You don't even have to
  read to answer. Find the part that matches and write it down. It is
  stupid stupid dumb boring."

- "Well, we read *Shiloh* and for each chapter we had ten questions to answer. I hated that."
- "You read it and so what?"

"*You read it and so what?*" That statement reminded us of Marcus's comment: "But, it's just like nothing we do there is going to change anything here." And there it is. In too many places, we ask kids to read (and write) so we can give them a grade that shows they've learned some skills someone has decided they need to learn. Skills are important. But if we aren't reading and writing so that we can grow, so that we can discover, so that we can change—change our thinking, change ourselves, perhaps help change the world—then those skills will be for naught.

From Extracting to Transacting

As we visited classrooms, we jotted down assignments we saw on white boards or on worksheets, or heard teachers give. Here's a sampling of what we collected:

- Write a summary
- Provide a retell
- Compare and contrast two characters/people/events
- List the steps
- Create a timeline
- Draw the parts of a cell
- Outline the chapter
- Cite the evidence
- Explain the main idea and supporting details
- Answer the questions
- Complete the plot structure template
- Define the vocabulary words
- Discuss the causes and effects

And if we're trying to be creative, we let kids make a diorama of their favorite scene.

All of those tasks are, at their core, about extracting. We would argue that in today's world, learning to extract information is not enough. It's not enough to hold a reader's interest and it's not enough to solve our complex problems. We need students who can do more than answer questions; today's complex world requires that our next generation of leaders be able to raise questions. They need to be able to hold multiple ideas in their minds. They need to be able to see a situation from multiple perspectives. They need to be flexible thinkers who recognize that there will rarely be one correct answer, but instead there will be multiple answers that must be weighed and evaluated. Yet, here we are in the second decade of the twenty-first century still focused on practices that teach students to extract evidence from a text. We ask students why Jess took Maybelle to Terabithia when we should be asking how Terabithia has changed their understanding of who they, the readers, are.

We think that knowing what the text says is critically important. It is a necessary part of the meaning-making experience, but it is not sufficient. Additionally, we must teach students how to read with curiosity. And they need to be willing to raise questions. We want them to ask not only, "What does this text say?" but also, "What does it say to me? How does it change who I am? How might it change what I do in the world?"

> **We need students who can do more than answer questions; today's complex world requires that our next generation of leaders be able to raise questions.**

Our next generation of leaders will lead us in many areas. Whether that person is leading one classroom of children or one community's police force or one local business or a state agency or our nation, our children of today must, most certainly, learn to think creatively, critically, collaboratively, and compassionately. To get there, we need them to change the way they think as they read. We need to change the readers they are.

Take Two: Chapter 1
scholastic.com/
BeersandProbst

Turn and Talk

A word about this section. First, by each Turn and Talk section at the end of each chapter, you'll see the URL scholastic.com/BeersandProbst. At that site, you can join us in an informal conversation about the topics in the chapter. Second, we urge you to find colleagues for your own conversation to discuss the questions offered here. Our goal is that they help you start conversations in your school. Some questions will require a few meetings to discuss. Others might not. Some might require anonymity to achieve the most honesty. So, perhaps you should address those in writing; the answers might then be collected and shared in a small-group setting. The best questions, of course, will come from you and your colleagues.

- How often do you ask your students, "How did this reading change who you are?" If not often, explore with colleagues why that is. Do you believe that reading can change who you are? If you do, then why not discuss that with students?

- We've heard some teachers say that in the future, reading may not be as important as it is now, since we will have more audio books and will be able to turn to the Internet to watch/listen to someone explain almost anything. Do you agree? Do you think in the future we'll read less? Is reading still necessary even now?

> *this is also "ready"*

- What will be lost if reading is less valued? How do you share the value of reading with students in your school?

- In this country, we kept slaves from learning to read. Additionally, for a while in our history, you were adequately literate if you could simply sign your name—or even just make an X. In developing countries today, girls are still educated less than boys. What do these situations suggest about the potential power of reading?

Chapter 2

The Responsive Reader

FOR KIDS TO BECOME the readers our ever-changing society needs—our *democracy* needs—the first thing they must do is become responsive readers.

The book—or poem, or editorial, or movie, or any other text—will offer the students nothing more than a task to be completed if all they are expected to do is decode correctly, retell completely, summarize accurately. It is only when they link that text to their own experiences that the text will begin to matter, and it may then evoke more rigorous attention, reflection, and analysis. When the text matters, when it plays a role in their intellectual, social, emotional, and physical worlds, then they are likely to do more than simply decode the words, simply call them out, simply repeat them, and perhaps simply try—probably futilely—to remember them. When the text matters to them, then we are on our way to having responsive readers.

But the text won't matter to them unless it touches them emotionally or intellectually. And so readers must be aware, not only of the text, but of the effects the text has upon them. They must be responsive. That means they must be alert to their own reactions to the text.

Alert to Their Own Responses

Benji: You have GOT to read *The True Story of the Three Little Pigs*. It is the funniest book ever. I LOVED it. (a first grader)

Sharon: When I was little, my mom would read *Corduroy* to me over and over and over. I don't know why I loved that book so

much but I did. It made me sad because *Corduroy* didn't have a home and then it made me happy because he did.
(a second grader)

Corin: Did it [the story] make me think about anything? Like what?
(a seventh grader)

RJ: Did it help me think about me in any way? I don't even know what that means. (a ninth grader)

When the reader notices what's going on inside himself and feels the emotion or raises the question that the text evokes, he is doing more than simply decoding, more than simply word calling, more than simply memorizing what the text offers him. He is instead opening himself up to the text, interacting with it, accepting its invitation into the fictional world or—if nonfiction—recognizing its intrusion into his world, and using it to help him make sense of his own experience.

This responsive reader is aware of the effects a text has upon her and the response it evokes—amusement, curiosity, surprise, revulsion, doubt, uncertainty, or any of countless other possible reactions. She will be awake to those possibilities, will notice those inner stirrings, and will think about them. Just as she notices the uncertain tremor of anxiety awakened in her by the frown on her teacher's face, the responsive reader will notice that uncertainty and doubt awakened in her by the frown on the face of the character in the novel. In both instances, she will pause and ask herself essentially, "What does my response—this anxiety or doubt I feel—tell me about what is happening in the world (with this frowning teacher) or in the text (with this frowning character)?"

> **For kids to become the readers our ever-changing society needs—our *democracy* needs—they must become responsive readers.**

This, we think, is what even the youngest child does quite naturally, at her own level, when someone reads her a story. She is aware of her curiosity. She wants to know what will happen next. Will the three bears find Goldilocks and what will happen to her? She is aware of her own anxiety. Will Chrysanthemum end up liking her name? Even these very simple stories awaken feelings and create expectations, and even the

While working with some eighth graders, one of us mentioned that reading ought to awaken inner stirrings. One boy responded a bit too enthusiastically, "Inner stirrings? Well, okay!" We decided not to use that phrase with adolescents again. Ever.

youngest child, though he may not be able to articulate them clearly, is aware of those stirrings in his own mind. It is our older readers, we worry, who seem to have learned to set aside their own responses entirely or to have relegated them to a lower status. As a student at Sam Houston State University said, "What is my response? Does that matter?"

The responsive reader is present, in mind and heart, when he is reading the text. Rather than simply collecting facts or trying to remember information that, unless it matters, will remain pointless, he is trying to *make sense*. It is much like what he does every day with the world around him. He observes, notices, and tries to make sense of what he sees. In the cafeteria, at lunch, he is unlikely to collect information at random. He doesn't count the number of students present, doesn't calculate the ratio of boys to girls, doesn't estimate the percentages of tall, short, and middling students. All of that information is there to be observed, noted, collected, and remembered, if there were any point to it. But to do so without some reason would simply be to undertake an exercise. It would be akin to the decoding of nonsense words we may ask of a student to merely demonstrate that he is able

to transform squiggles on the page into sounds that hang together. Instead, he looks around the cafeteria and takes in and makes sense of information that matters to him.

When readers are lost in a book, they stand a good chance of finding themselves.

That student might enter the cafeteria and sense that it "feels different." If so, he is being alert to his own responses. He might then look around and notice that this feeling may have been evoked by an unusually large number of empty tables, and then he may wonder, "What accounts for this? Where is everyone?" Aware of his response to the feeling of strangeness the half-empty room evoked, he is motivated to make sense of that feeling by raising questions about it and collecting the observations that may answer them. And so, awareness of his responses should lead to a close look at what has caused them—in other words, to the room itself or, if he is reading, to the text itself. Just as he observes the teacher's frown, senses the growing discomfort it has caused him to feel; just as he observes the cafeteria, senses that it seems strange, and then attempts to figure out what it means; so, too, does he read the words on the page, sense the reaction they evoke, and then attempt to figure out what his reaction to those words might mean.

Alert to the Responses of Other Readers

Additionally, the responsive reader might be, *should be*, responsive to the thoughts and reactions of other readers. Without a text, a student is limited to her own perceptions and insights. With the text, she has the benefit of interaction, if she accepts the invitation, with one other person—the author—and perhaps more if we accept the characters as others. But if she collaborates with a group, a small group within her class, or perhaps the entire class, then she has the rich resources of many minds brought to bear upon the same text.

That same text, entering different minds, will yield different readings. Each of us is unduplicated, bringing to the text a unique personality, a unique set of expectations and hopes, a unique personal history. Consequently, what we make of the text will be unique. Shaped by our idiosyncrasies, our readings will differ, even if only slightly, from one another. The text broadens and enriches the individual's experience; talking about it with others broadens and enriches the individual's otherwise limited and narrow insight still further.

The talk in the classroom is thus very important. It enables us both to see aspects of the text that we did not manage to perceive when

If you haven't read Ellin Keene's book *Talk About Understanding*, add it to your must-read list.

trapped within our own isolated minds, and to see something about ourselves that would go unobserved if not for the comparison of our reading with the readings of others. A book such as *Bully* by Patricia Polacco, which, as the title suggests, is about bullying, explicitly calls for the comparison of our reading and yours by ending with the question, addressed to the readers, "What would you do?"

This question allows the readers to discuss how people, either victims or witnesses, might react to bullying. The talk might first be about the character. Should she return to the school or leave it and go to another school? It is easy to imagine those students who would more courageously or defiantly argue that the character should return to the school and confront her tormentor. Others would probably say it's safer and wiser to leave that school and go to a more comfortable place. Each reader brings his own history, his own language, values, and worldviews, to the text. Some may have been victims of bullying themselves; others may have perpetrated the crime upon their classmates; still others may have witnessed it and tried to ignore it; a few may have witnessed it and tried to intervene. All of those readers will have different comments to offer about the story. Hearing those different reactions will enrich and sharpen the readings of each. Without the responses and thoughts of other readers, the isolated reader has only his own resources to draw upon.

> **If the reader isn't responsive, if she doesn't let the text awaken emotion or inspire thoughts, then she can barely be said to be reading at all.**

But It Begins With Responsiveness

If the reader isn't responsive, if she doesn't let the text awaken emotion or inspire thoughts, then she can barely be said to be reading at all. Passing her eyes across the page, collecting undigested bits of information from the text, preparing to answer recall questions about it, even committing parts of it to memory, can scarcely be compared with the richer activity of responding emotionally and intellectually to the words on the page, looking inside oneself to see what lies there, examining the text to see what caused those reactions, and sharing perceptions and understandings with other readers.

Turn and Talk

Take Two: Chapter 2
scholastic.com/
BeersandProbst

- In workshops, we've occasionally had teachers tell us that they don't care how students respond to a text. "My job is to teach them to understand it." Our point is that responsiveness is critical for understanding, even more critical for close reading. What is your thinking about the role of responsiveness?

- You might reconsider the opening sentence: "For kids to become the readers our ever-changing society needs—our *democracy* needs—they must become responsive readers." Do you and your colleagues agree with this statement?

- What's happening in your classrooms and in your school to encourage responsive reading?

Chapter 3

The Responsible Reader

OBVIOUSLY, THE READER'S RESPONSIVENESS to her own feelings is necessary but insufficient, just as we know the ability to decode is necessary but insufficient. It is the response that connects the reader to the text and demands that she attend to the words on the page. The responsive reader must also be a responsible reader.

She must do more than simply respond. She must—if she is to be responsible—examine the feelings awakened by the text. She should question the thoughts of her own that the text has called to mind, assess the writer's evidence and logic, speculate about his purposes and his biases, and finally come to some reasoned and responsible conclusions about the text and her reading of it. The response is the beginning, but only the beginning.

If the text is to provide anything beyond idle amusement, a distraction from the tasks and problems that confront us, or—worse—a way for others to manipulate us, then there must be an element of responsibility in the act of reading.

It's pointless to collect information if you do nothing with it. It contributes nothing to your intellectual or emotional growth to notice that you have responded in a particular way to a text, but not give the significance of that response any further thought. It is a waste of time to hear what someone says about a text and then to either reject it out of hand or accept it uncritically. If the text is to provide anything beyond idle amusement, a distraction from the tasks and problems that confront us, or—worse—a way for others to manipulate us, then there must be an element of responsibility in the act of reading.

Responsibility to the Text

Take a look at two conversations, the first between sixth graders.

Brendon: Why did it say, "It was a metal thing"?

Sharon: It didn't say that. He's in the wilderness. There isn't any metal. Except his hatchet. Was it talking about his hatchet?

Brendon: No. But it did too say it was a metal thing. See right here. Page 98. Oh. Wait. It says, "It was a mental thing." Oh. That's really different.

And now this one between fifth graders...

Lila: That article, about the left-behind children in China. I didn't know anything about that.

Ellie: Me neither. I thought it was good that the Chinese government was going to try to do something.

Lila: They won't do anything.

Ellie: That's not what it said.

Lila: That doesn't matter. Just because the government says they are doing something doesn't mean anything.

One aspect of responsibility, and the one that has perhaps been most heavily emphasized by state standards, is responsibility to the text. While we, of course, want students who pay attention to what's in the text, we know that the most responsible reading requires that students pay attention to their own responses, their own thoughts, their own reactions. Responsible reading is rooted in a reader's response, and that response attends to both the words on the page and the thoughts the reader brings with her.

Yet, the attention to the reader's response has sometimes been seen as a dismissal of the words on the page. Fearing that, some advocate encouraging students to focus their attention on what is there, in print, on the page. If a response should be offered, it is, too often, seen as an unimportant idea, one to be heard and then discounted.

These students are discussing a line from Chapter 11 of *Hatchet* by Gary Paulsen.

These students are discussing an article from the September 5, 2016, issue of *Junior Scholastic* titled "China's Left-Behind Children."

PART I

We share some of our favorite strategies that help students focus on the text on pages 64–65.

Reading responsibly requires attending to what's on the page. Such attention does not mean the reader's responses should be relegated to mere opinion. Both what's on the page and what's in the head are important. Focusing on the reader to the neglect of the text, or focusing on the text to the neglect of the reader, is problematic. To encourage and expect nothing more of students than unexamined statements of feelings is to encourage intellectual laziness. And to encourage only extracting of information, memorizing of details, and the like, is to reduce reading to an unrewarding exercise.

In an effort to encourage responsible attention to the text, the profession has sometimes allowed us to reduce the reader to a subordinate, and almost insignificant, position. In an effort to encourage students to read carefully and closely, we may have suggested that the reader's job is little more than that of extracting, accepting, and assimilating what the text offers. It seems to us that responsibility to the text might be differently conceived.

Bob listens as this student explains what in the text caused her response.

Certainly it involves trying to figure out and acknowledge what the text says. To impute to the text any assertions it does not make is simply to perpetrate a fraud. To deny or ignore assertions that the text does make is equally irresponsible. Those intellectual failings become more obvious—and dangerous—when confronting significant issues. Texts dealing with human rights, climate change, clean water, and other such important matters may have great consequence in our lives. They merit serious and responsible attention. And to think our students don't consider such issues is wrong. In Chapter 12, we share tough issues students want to discuss. Our democracy is best served when we encourage students to begin at an early age to pay close attention both to what the text says and to what they feel and think as they read. Not one or the other, but both.

> To impute to the text any assertions it does not make is simply to perpetrate a fraud. To deny or ignore assertions that the text does make is equally irresponsible.

Learning to Question the Text

What we see is that our young readers are inclined not to question a text. Parents and teachers and other adults they trust tell them things they need to know. Why wouldn't a text do the same? Consider this conversation with a second grader. He's discussing an article he just read titled "Are Trampolines Dangerous?"

Kylene: What did the author decide? Are trampolines too dangerous to jump on?

Darius: I think it said too dangerous.

Kylene: Why is that?

Darius: It said that the little girl broke her tooth. And now her parents won't let her jump on her friend's trampoline. My friend has a trampoline and my parents won't let me jump on it. They say it is too dangerous. They heard about a boy, he was jumping, and he fell off and now he can't walk.

Kylene: Did the author mention how to make jumping on a trampoline safer?

Darius: [Darius looks back through the text.] Yes. You can just have one person jump at a time. And no flips.

Kylene: So, does this author think they are safe to jump on?

Darius: They aren't. You can't jump on them.

Kylene: I agree with your opinion and what your parents have told you. But does the author have an opinion?

Darius: He thinks they are bad.

Kylene: What about this section where he discusses how to make jumping on them be safer?

Darius: I don't know. Maybe he is saying they *could* be safe. I think the author maybe he doesn't know.

Darius is young and he's just beginning to learn how to examine a text. We aren't concerned that it took a nudge for him to recognize that his opinion of the danger level of trampolines wasn't emphatically shared by the author. Asking younger students to critically examine their response requires we stay alert to the comments they make. When students make assertions that are not supported by the text, rephrasing those comments and asking them to find support in the text help them understand what's in the text and what is not. It's far too easy, for children and adults, to add to the text what is not there. Asking for evidence to support a response is always important.

> **Our democracy is best served when we encourage students to begin at an early age to pay close attention both to what the text says and to what they feel and think as they read. Not one or the other, but both.**

We're more concerned with the following conversation with a fourth grader about an article regarding headphones and loud music. This student has decided what the author believes based solely on what he, the reader, thinks.

In this article ("Doctor Says It's Best to Keep Volume at Medium or Lower with Ear Buds"), an ear surgeon outlines the pros and cons of three types of headphones that people wear while listening to music. His final conclusion is that there are benefits and problems with all types of headphones and the best thing to do is to keep music at a low volume.

Kylene: Did anything surprise you about what Dr. Pearlman said?

Luke: I was surprised that he said it doesn't matter if you wear headphones or ear buds. They are both okay.

Kylene: Did Dr. Pearlman say they are both okay?

Luke: Yeah. They are both okay.

Kylene: Can you show me where it says that?

Luke: It says, "Pearlman can't tell patients what kinds of headphones to use."

Kylene: What does the next sentence say?

Luke: "All of them have different benefits and problems."

Kylene: Did you read the different benefits and downsides?

Luke: He doesn't say don't wear ear buds so I wear mine.

Kylene: What did he say about the volume of music?

Luke: He doesn't like music.

Kylene: I didn't see that. Where did you find that?

Luke: Well, he says to keep the volume down.

Kylene: Right.

Luke: Everyone who likes music likes loud music.

Luke's opinion about the value of loud music was so strong that he drew conclusions about Dr. Pearlman that the text did not support. While Darius was willing to distinguish between what the text says and what he thought, Luke was not. We aren't asking readers to let go of their own opinions, but we do want them to recognize the distinction between what they bring to the text and what the text has brought to them. And, when warranted, we want them to be willing to change their minds. When readers are aware of the contribution both they and the text make, comments might look like this:

- This word caused my confusion.

- This assertion caused me to distrust the author.

- This allayed my doubts and convinced me that the author may be right.

- This makes me suspect of the author's intentions.

Okay. We know of no elementary-aged child, well, actually no child of any age, who will use this language. Here's what you're more likely to hear and how you might respond:

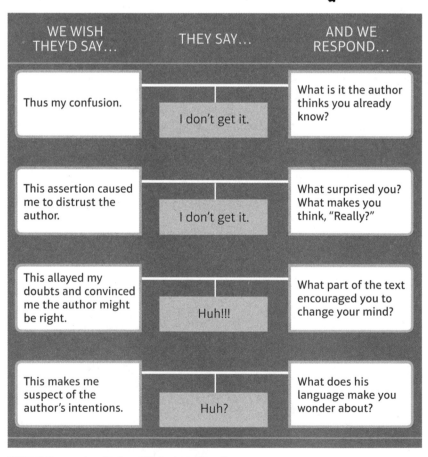

WE WISH THEY'D SAY...	THEY SAY...	AND WE RESPOND...
Thus my confusion.	I don't get it.	What is it the author thinks you already know?
This assertion caused me to distrust the author.	I don't get it.	What surprised you? What makes you think, "Really?"
This allayed my doubts and convinced me the author might be right.	Huh!!!	What part of the text encouraged you to change your mind?
This makes me suspect of the author's intentions.	Huh?	What does his language make you wonder about?

CHART B Conversations We Have With Students About Texts

We encourage this responsibility to the text by asking kids to keep three big questions in mind.

- What surprised me?
- What did the author think I already know?
- What changed, challenged, or confirmed my thinking?

These prompts most certainly require that students think about their own responses, but they are responses that come directly from the text. Don't be reluctant to ask children to "Show me what in the text caused that surprise" or "Where did the author need to tell you more?"

Heidi Weber shared her Three Big Questions sketch notes with us.

Responsibility to Oneself

That close attention to the words—the responsibility a reader shows to the text—implies and requires a responsibility to oneself as well as the words on the page. That responsibility consists not only of a willingness to acknowledge and defend one's own thoughts and values, but to change thinking when evidence or reason dictates. A second grader, who read a text about the critical importance of bees in the food chain, adamantly contended, "I don't like bees because they sting. We don't need them." His strong feelings about bees led him to dismiss what he might have learned if he had read more responsibly. Equally irresponsible is the third grader who read about climate change and responded, "I don't believe in it. My friend said it isn't real." If that child wants to argue with the science presented in the article, that's one thing. But to dismiss the article because it contradicts what a friend has previously stated is not responsible reading.

Take Two: Three Big Questions

Join us as we discuss the Three Big Questions in more detail: scholastic.com/ BeersandProbst

Our students are not too young to learn to respect both the words on the page and their own thoughts and values. We seldom have difficulty persuading them to hang on tightly to their own ideas. They come to class, too often, ready to assert that whatever they think, whatever they have come to believe, is flatly, simply, indisputably true and correct. They are often much more willing to defend their thoughts than to reconsider and perhaps modify them. And they should, of course,

> **But to hold on to ideas when evidence and reason suggest that a change is sensible is to fail to be responsible to oneself.**

defend and protect what is reasoned and defensible. But to hold on to ideas when evidence and reason suggest that a change is sensible is to fail to be responsible to oneself. Somehow, we need to teach them to value change. Not change for change's sake, but change that results from more information, a richer understanding, a sharpened perspective.

They should begin learning, as early as possible, not to misrepresent the text. To do so is to fail in their responsibility to the text, certainly, but even more significantly it is to fail in their responsibility to themselves. To assert that the text says what it does not say, or that it does not say what it, in fact, does say, is to deny themselves the opportunity to think or to learn. Regardless of their age, students are not too young to learn to defend their position when it is defensible and to change it when new information, insight, or reasoning persuades them.

Responsibility to Others

The apparent increase in what has come to be called "fake news" makes the issue of responsibility to others even more important. It has perhaps always been easy to allow ourselves to be led astray by inaccurate or dishonest texts, especially when our emotions are aroused.

If we find that a text angers us, or, on the other hand, greatly pleases us, then we are likely to react quickly, perhaps without checking to see if either the anger or the pleasure is warranted. Now, however, not only can we be led astray by irresponsible texts, but we have the capacity, through social media, to help that text lead hundreds or thousands of others astray. The simple act of retweeting or sharing something online can vastly compound and extend the damage.

News: Fake or Real?

We could spend chapters discussing the differences between news that is reported and news that is invented; in parsing the difference between false and fake. We could take up the struggles that social media sites now face as they decide how to avoid promoting fake news without acting as self-appointed censors. Our right to free speech is a valued freedom in this country and any group that decides to ban this news or that news because the site is deemed "fake" will face scrutiny. The lines between satire, bias, humor, falsehood, and deceit, and how a text is labeled, will grow blurrier as news sources worry more about high ratings than reliable reporting.

Satire has, of course, been a part of our discourse for a long time and most of us have probably had the unsettling experience of momentarily being taken in by something in *The Onion* or by a Borowitz tongue-in-cheek column. There is some satisfaction in seeing

> **Where the writer of satire relies on the reader's intelligence and skepticism, the writer of fake news seems to rely instead on the reader's gullibility and laziness.**

through the satirist's invention to the truth that lies beneath it or behind it. The satirist expects the reader to be sharp enough to see the joke, recognize the exaggeration and invention, laugh at the humor in it all, and not be corrupted or misled by the fictitious elements.

Fake news, however, seems to have gone one or two steps further. It has moved across the line from humorous exaggeration intended to amuse and promote thought, into lies and deceptions quite likely intended to make the author money by inviting readers to click on the site and therefore attracting advertisers (Dewey, 2014; Silverman, 2016). Where the writer of satire relies on the reader's intelligence and skepticism, the writer of fake news seems to rely instead on the reader's gullibility and laziness.

Whatever the writer's motivations may be, the reader clearly bears the responsibility for avoiding gullibility and laziness. If the reader is taken in by invented news stories, he has obviously failed himself. And if he participates in circulating them, through sharing, reacting, and commenting, then he has failed in his responsibility to others.

Social Media and the News

Responsible reading of the news is more critical now than ever before because so much of the news we all read comes to us from social media sites. In 2016, 62 percent of U.S. adults reported they get at least some of their news from social media, with 18 percent saying all their news comes from social media (Pew Research Center, 2016). We know there are days when we are part of that 18 percent. We're fast out the door in

the morning, quick into a school with kids or a workshop with teachers, then off to an airplane to do it again the next day in another city. If the plane has an Internet connection, we log on and try to catch up on what's been happening in the world. Reddit, Facebook, and Twitter become our window to the universe.

On those days, we've discovered that there was a missing Red Rump Tarantula in Brooklyn; that Tim Horton's will stop serving pork due to Muslim demands; that Pope Francis endorsed Trump for President; that a protester at a Trump rally was paid $3,500. All of those stories, *all* of them, were fake. They were indeed "stories." We both fell for one of them as we wondered just what would happen when that Red Rump Tarantula had her babies, which was the reason the owner gave for posting the warning signs about her throughout a certain area of Brooklyn.

On social media sites, the "news" is quickly disseminated. We may see that 3.5K have shared it, another 1K have commented, and that it's trending. Surely all those people can't be duped. This story must be the real thing. The danger in assuming that the story is real means we must put more effort into the reading of news; we must work harder, something that's tough to do at the end of a long day. But we can't look at a news item and presume truth. Instead, we must come to news ready to sort, to cull, to mull, to test, to confirm, to question, to challenge, to discard—and that's in addition to just reading the content. If we don't, we find ourselves wondering if that escaped tarantula in Brooklyn could find itself in Texas or Florida. If fake news writers are counting on people to be dumb, then we must be smart. We must muster the stamina to be responsible.

You can find the fake news story about the tarantula at scholastic.com/ BeersandProbst.

Helping Kids Spot Fake News

Perhaps rather than wondering which story we should approach skeptically   this one yes, that one no—we might teach our readers to do three things as they look at any news stories, especially when they begin to look at stories online. Let's teach them to ask themselves:

- How does it look?
- What does it say?
- How does it make me feel?

How Does It Look?

When we ask kids to think about how a story looks, we want them checking out the headlines, the photos, and the URL. All caps in headlines, or headlines filled with extreme language, photos that present unlikely information, and URLs that don't end in .com, .gov, .edu, .org, or .net are worth reconsidering. For example, the URL abcnews.com.co takes us to a source of fake news. That ".co" ending should raise a red flag. A quick search of "how to identify fake URLs" will show you several articles that help you learn to identify fake website addresses.

What Does It Say?

When we ask students to think about what the news story says, we want them to ask themselves questions about the topic, about the language, and about the author. If the topic doesn't seem credible, it might not be. We should have realized that a story about a lost pregnant tarantula just didn't seem right. Or if the language is extreme, then there's probably a problem. And if the author can't be found or there's a name but you can't find out information about the author, think twice before sharing.

How Does It Make You Feel?

Finally, when we ask students to think about how the article makes them feel, we want them to be aware of particular responses: If it makes them excessively angry, scared, or, on the other hand, reaffirmed and smug, then they ought to do some checking before sharing.

When students begin to read news stories wondering how it looks, what it says, and how it makes them feel, we tell them that if any response raises a concern, then the first thing they should do is step away from the share button! Next, they should look to see if other news sources are reporting the same information. If not, then they should not trust the story. Or,

> Until we teach students to read responsibly, we run the risk of being a nation of readers who not only harm themselves, but potentially harm others as they share not just misinformation but blatant lies.

they can head to a source such as Snopes.com to see if the information can be verified.

Until we teach students to read responsibly, we run the risk of being a nation of readers who not only harm themselves, but potentially harm others as they share not just misinformation but blatant lies.

Turn and Talk

Take Two: Chapter 3
scholastic.com/
BeersandProbst

- Would you and your colleagues say that responsibility in reading must be both to the text and to oneself, or exclusively to the text?

- What's the result for our society if we fail to raise readers who are both responsive and responsible?

- How much are you influenced by fake news? What's happening in your school to help teach your students how to critically evaluate news sources?

- Would you say that the spread of fake news is a threat to our democracy?

Chapter 4

The Compassionate Reader

As we visited a fourth-grade classroom, we overhead this conversation:

Kayla: That's not fair.

Teacher: Well, I'm sorry, but I told the class that if anyone was late then everyone would go late to recess.

Kayla: But it's not fair. *I* wasn't late. This is all Marlena's fault. She is ruining recess.

Shayna: Shhh, Kayla. You're making Marlena feel terrible. Just be quiet.

Kayla: [whispering] Okay. But it's not fair.

We share that anecdote not to raise questions about the teacher's tactics for trying to get all students back in their seats after they returned from music class; nor do we want to encourage a conversation about Kayla's frustration. It was Shayna's comments that caught our attention. This fourth grader set aside her own feelings to instead see the moment through Marlena's eyes. She felt compassion for Marlena and hushed her other friend. We want that student in more classrooms.

It would be hard to argue against the goal of creating more compassionate people in our schools, though some would argue that teaching values does not belong in a school setting. Others would say that compassion can't be measured and tested and therefore should not take instructional time. We agree that it is hard to measure. We would hate to see the multiple-choice test designed to measure an individual's capacity to show compassion. We can imagine horrid scenes with ridiculous A, B, C, and D options from which to choose. We can see compassion being reduced to a series of objectives: *The student will define compassion. The student will compare and contrast compassion and empathy. The student will demonstrate compassion, give examples of compassion in a variety of contexts, and provide supporting evidence.* We worry about the language of a compassion standard: "Act compassionately, proficiently, and independently at grade level." Heaven help us. Yes, in many ways, we're happier if we keep compassion—as a goal—out of the curriculum.

And yet, we need it there. The last few years—and particularly the 2016 Presidential election year—have shown us brutality, racism, sexism, misogyny; hateful language and acts toward members of the LGBTQ community; increased bullying in schools; vitriolic language and unsubstantiated assertions via Twitter, personal blogs, YouTube videos, and online news sources. Because the Internet allows a level of anonymity, some people may feel "safe" being vulgar, dismissive, and hurtful. But the words are still there and the impact—whether inflicted by an unknown person or a prominent political figure—is still painful.

We think that developing more compassionate citizens is a desirable goal in and of itself. But not only is compassion a desirable characteristic

> Compassion should sharpen the readers' ability to see other points of view, other perspectives, and to imagine the feelings of those who hold them.

of people, we also think that it is a necessary characteristic of readers. The more capable readers are of compassion, the more likely it is that they will be able to read well. Compassion should sharpen the readers' ability to see other points of view, other perspectives, and to imagine the feelings of those who hold them. It should enable readers to take, if only momentarily, the perspective of someone else and thus better understand motivations and thinking.

But to be willing to take on another's perspective or perhaps to let the author present you with an idea you are predisposed to reject, you first must be willing to enter the text. You must be willing to enter into a dialogue with the text, to interact and not merely extract. And through these transactions with texts, we might learn how to better enter into conversations with those in the real world who offer us another perspective or present us with an idea we are reluctant to hear. As we learn to read our books, we might better learn to read the world.

Choosing Not to Read

We suggest that we've failed to become a nation of readers in part because we have made reading a painful exercise for kids. High-stakes tests, Lexile levels, searches for evidence, dialogic notes, and sticky notes galore—we have demanded of readers many things we would never do ourselves while reading. We have sticky-noted reading to death.

Seriously, as you finished the book you most recently enjoyed, did you pause, hold the book gently in your hands, and say to yourself, "This time, *this time*, I think I'll make a diorama"? Or, perhaps on that cold Friday night with wine in hand when you finally had thirty minutes to yourself, you relaxed in your favorite chair, picked up that newest book you've been aching to read, and then shot out of that comfortable spot to retrieve your spiral notebook so you could record unknown vocabulary words. Did you finish that interesting article on the global water shortage, then call your friend so she could ask you ten multiple-choice questions about the text? Do you write summaries of what you read, make new book jackets, rewrite the ending, take tests over every text? Any text? Do you want your reading level put on a bulletin board for all to see? Do you even *know* your damn reading level?

While there is no single template for the aliterate reader, there are some frequently repeated comments from the students who can read but choose not to do so. One is that "reading is boring." In other words,

> High stakes tests, Lexile levels, searches for evidence, dialogic notes, and sticky notes galore—we have demanded of readers many things we would never do ourselves while reading. We have sticky-noted reading to death.

when we look at all we have done to what should be a pleasurable act, we think that what students, if more eloquent, might be saying is that we've taken the personal out of reading; we've made the reading of fiction and nonfiction about extracting. We have, while racing to the top, lowered our students' vision of all that reading can be.

Stances: Aesthetic and Efferent

Too often, we fear we have abandoned the aesthetic aspect of reading and turned it almost entirely into an efferent task. In other words, we may have encouraged our students to forget about themselves while reading, to ignore what the text does to their thoughts and their emotions in an effort to get them to extract information, facts, details—all of that concrete data that can be memorized though it may not be memorable—from the text. Our students have finished *The Giver* and we have asked, "What assignment did Asher receive?" While reading *The Watsons Go to Birmingham–1963*, they have hidden behind the couch with Kenny after walking through the bombed-out church with him and then we have asked, "What significance did the black shoe hold for Kenny?" They have finished *The One and Only Ivan* and we have asked them who Ruby was and how she met Ivan.

They have read of children forced into labor situations akin to slavery and we ask them to compare and contrast conditions in Costa Rica with conditions in Ecuador. They have read about Garana, the girl who walks to a mosque each morning alone to say her prayers, and we have asked them to define the word "mosque." We have turned the aesthetic act into an efferent one, and in doing so we may have encouraged them to ignore themselves and focus almost entirely on what they find on the page.

Efferent and *aesthetic* are Louise Rosenblatt's words (1938/1995). She said that when we read aesthetically, we are aware of ourselves and of the effects the text is having upon us. We may vicariously experience the action in the text; become the character or the person; lose ourselves to the experiences in the book. We may find the text awakening feelings or raising questions. Whatever the effect may be, if we are reading "aesthetically," we are aware of it. We may make a conscious choice about

Several of our favorite articles for children about child labor and children in refugee camps can be found at scholastic.com/ BeersandProbst.

whether to explore those reactions or not. If the recipe we are reading reminds us of our grandmother, we choose either to enjoy the memory or return to the oven. But the point is, we choose. If the memories are pleasant, we may indulge them. We may even modify our recipe slightly, remembering how our grandmother would have done it. If the cake begins to burn, however, we'll abandon those memories and remind ourselves we should have paid more attention to the temperature prescribed on the page. Whatever effect the text has on us, if we are reading "aesthetically," we are alert to what the text is doing to us.

By contrast, when we read efferently, we are reading to extract information from the text. We probably should read the instructions for completing our income tax forms efferently. We read the orders for how to take that new blood pressure medicine efferently. One of us read aesthetically multiple ways for roasting a turkey, calling to mind past turkey dinners and helpful hints from her grandmother on how to baste to perfection. The other encouraged a faster, efferent reading so he could eat the turkey sooner rather than later. Yes, there are times when extracting information is all we need to do. When the plane is going down and we pull out the laminated sheet of instructions telling us where the emergency door is and how to open it (and reminding us to kiss our computer bags goodbye), none of us want to linger over the eloquent language—all we want to do is grab the information and run, or exit down the slide. We want to seize that information correctly, accurately, completely, but that's all. We want the purely efferent experience of extracting the data so that we'll be around to have an aesthetic experience, probably with another text, tomorrow.

But if efferent reading is all we teach kids, if we convince them that reading is only for extracting, then we will have failed to teach them that texts are not simply repositories of facts. They are instead the catalysts for an experience that may involve emotions and thoughts of our own. Reading gives us an opportunity to have an intimate conversation with the text, with the author, with oneself, and then ultimately with others. And it is those conversations, all of them, that might be enriched by compassionate thinking.

Bob: Kylene thinks cookbooks offer times for exploration, moments to reflect, places to put notes on how the meal was enjoyed.

Kylene: Bob is actually amazed to discover that cookbooks are a genre.

Chapter 4

Compassion and Nonfiction

It's easy to think of developing compassion as we read fiction, but compassion plays a role, as well, in the reading of nonfiction. If our stance toward a situation or an event that we might encounter in readings in history or science is utterly without concern, without any feeling, it's hard to imagine that the reading will matter to us. Although nonfiction doesn't present us with imagined characters whose feelings and thoughts may be better understood by the compassionate reader, it does require us to engage in similar intellectual exertions.

It may, for instance, require us to imagine and understand the motivations of people offering perspectives outside our own. The Scholastic Scope article "Growing Up Muslim in Post 9/11 America" offers non-Muslim readers the chance to consider what it means to be labeled a terrorist simply because of one's religion. In *Rachel Carson: Fighting Pesticides and Other Chemical Pollutants*, young readers learn facts, most certainly, but they also have the chance to consider our "advances" in ridding crops of insects, and to do so from a broader perspective that takes into consideration how pesticides harm the natural world. When a group of middle-schoolers read *Up Before Daybreak*, a detailed account of the rise of the cotton industry, one student told us, "There were lots of dates but I just kept thinking about the parents who made their little kids, like six-year-olds, work all day long and then kept their money. I wanted to do something to help them and I kept wondering why someone didn't make them stop."

> **Nonfiction should not suggest nonfeeling. Nonfiction offers us the chance to learn not only about the world and the people in it, but about ourselves.**

Nonfiction should not suggest nonfeeling. Nonfiction offers us the chance to learn not only about the world and the people in it, but about ourselves. Nonfiction should matter. It mattered enough to the writer that he took the time to write it. It should matter to any reader who takes the time to read it. And that mattering consists of both feeling and thinking about it. A reader who is encouraged to read nonfiction from an aesthetic stance and not merely the efferent stance will become an empathetic and compassionate reader. This compassionate reader will be better able to imagine the feelings and the perspectives of author and people, better able to envision the human consequences of information or of choices made on the basis of that information.

Yes, aesthetic reading offers us the opportunity to get lost in the text and, while we are lost, perhaps to find ourselves. But if our questions lead students to merely extracting and if our primary goal is to check for the understanding that can be measured by how much they are able to remember, then children learn—text after text, year after year—that reading is simply for answering, for extracting, for telling. It is not for *becoming*. And we will, for yet another year, not become a nation of readers.

Transforming Reading to Transform the Reader

The reader we hope will graduate from our schools is one who is open to the possibility of change. To read with a commitment to remaining untouched, unmoved, unchanged is simply to waste one's time. New information, new arguments, new perspectives should offer the reader the possibility of sharpening and improving his thinking. This seems to be true whether that reader is thinking about the issues fiction often addresses—courage, loss, love, hate, and all of the others—or about the issues that nonfiction often raises—climate change, race relations, bullying, poverty, and all the others.

Granted, not every text will change us. Some, perhaps many, will confirm what we already thought without offering us anything new or different. But if we approach the text with determination to ignore or reject everything it may offer, there is little sense in approaching it at all.

So we have to produce readers who enter a text with compassion. Such a reader will be at the very least willing to consider the thoughts and feelings of characters he meets in fiction. He may conclude by rejecting or condemning some characters—in fact, we probably hope that he will. But he will begin by looking honestly at them. Such a reader, a compassionate reader, will approach the nonfiction text with openness, willing to consider the perspectives, motives, reasoning, and evidence he finds there. Again, he may conclude by rejecting the text, but if he rejects it before encountering it, he can hardly be said to have read it at all, even if his eyes have passed over every word. But if we can convince our students to read with compassion, perhaps they will begin to act with compassion. And perhaps, as adults, they will enter into conversations with one another with more civility, with more generosity, with more kindness toward one another.

Students take time to listen to buddies tell them why a book is important to them.

Turn and Talk

- We rarely think of reading as encouraging compassion and if we do, it is usually not discussed. Why do you think that is? Do you think encouraging compassion has a place in school?

- Do you think the reading of nonfiction offers students the chance to develop a compassionate nature? What examples would you offer that support your thinking?

- As we discussed this idea of compassion with one group of teachers, one teacher reported to us, "It's a nice idea, but it's really none of my business if my students (sixth graders) are compassionate or not. That's up to their parents to instill. My job is to teach them math and science." How would you respond to this teacher?

Take Two: Chapter 4
scholastic.com/
BeersandProbst

PART II
THE
FRAMEWORK
WE USE

Opening Comments

JEFF, A THIRD-YEAR TEACHER, asked us a question that stayed with us a long time. He had attended a workshop during which we discussed signposts discussed in our book *Notice and Note*. After the workshop, he spent time talking with us.

Jeff: I like these signposts, but where do they fit?

Bob: What do you mean?

Jeff: Where am I supposed to teach them? Where do they fit in the whole picture of reading?

Jeff is the very sort of teacher we hope stays in the profession for many years. He is excited to learn; he wants the best for his seventh graders; and he's trying to connect everything in his own thinking so he can connect it for his kids.

Jeff: I think my first two years, well, especially my first year, I was just throwing things at kids. "Hey, kids, let's do this!" I'm not sure I understood how everything I was trying to teach—strategies, standards, content—all fit together. I am sure they didn't either. I had this one kid last year, after we had spent two weeks talking about visualizing, who asked "So, are we still supposed to be visualizing?" FAIL. Me, not the kid. And then I read *Notice and Note*. I realized that as kids were noticing things, it would help them visualize. I had read another book that made it sound like you teach visualizing separately. I just need a way to make it all hang together.

We think Jeff is sharing a frustration many of us feel. Just where does this new thing I've learned fit into what I'm trying to do? Perhaps part of the problem is that we try to hand kids so much. Burt, a seventh grader, would support that idea.

We love Jeff's honesty about those first couple of years. We've often remarked that we should find our students from our first year of teaching and pay them. They taught us more than we taught them, we're sure.

Burt: Is this another strategy?

Kylene: What do you mean?

Burt: It's like every time you go to a conference you come back with something new we have to learn. Couldn't we just stick with what we're already doing?

Burt had a point. We (meaning the two of us) do have to watch our tendency to make sure kids aren't overwhelmed with strategies. We are positive that teachers often think, "Please, not one more new thing." Teachers are bombarded with "new" all the time. Districts adopt new practices, mandate new evaluation standards (for teachers and kids), take on new initiatives, require new textbooks, introduce new technology, add new kids, make new demands. Rarely, actually not ever, have we visited a district in which teachers have complained that there isn't enough "new" to do. No. The more common complaint is that each year they are inundated with new things to add while nothing is ever deleted.

So, Jeff's comments make sense to us. Where does anything new fit? In this part of the book, we want to show you an organizing principle. A framework. A simple (but not simplistic) way to nurture that responsive, responsible, and compassionate reader we need.

Chapter 5

Reading and Change

RESPONSIVE, RESPONSIBLE, AND COMPASSIONATE
reading might ultimately help us create the readers a democracy
requires. We've tried testing more; testing harder; testing longer. We've
raised the rigor, raised the Lexile, and raised the anxiety level around
high-stakes tests. We've rewritten standards, revised those rewritten
standards, and questioned all standards. We've brought into our
classrooms big books, little books, audio books, high-interest books,
and leveled books, and still we have too many kids who leave each
year without having read one single book, some bragging about that
accomplishment. Too many students still seem to think of books as
burdens imposed upon them, rather than as invitations to experience
new thoughts.

We have, over the decades, with great intensity, taught our students
decoding, fluency, and the process of extracting data from texts, but
perhaps we have not helped them understand the potential power of
the text in their own lives. While the kids who grow up as avid readers
understand at least the potential pleasure of reading, too few seem to
understand the power of reading to reshape themselves. In the 2015
Kids and Family Reading Report, when parents were asked how they
thought reading benefits their child, their most common responses
included developing vocabulary, improving imagination, and aiding in
school success. But nothing about helping kids reshape their own lives
(see Chart D).

Students enter schools that are test-driven, data-focused, and
Lexile-leveled, and learn that reading is too often simply the task of
remembering information. We hope that they will encounter teachers—
you are probably one of them—who show them the power of reading to
change their minds, change their thinking, and thus change themselves.

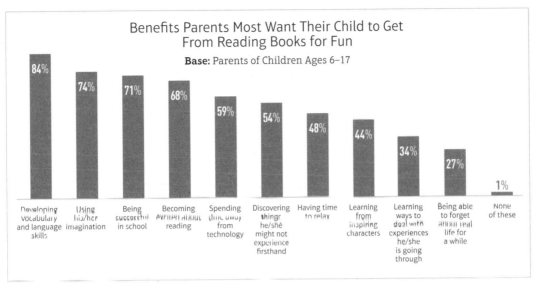

Benefits Parents Most Want Their Child to Get From Reading Books for Fun

Base: Parents of Children Ages 6–17

- 84% Developing vocabulary and language skills
- 74% Using his/her imagination
- 71% Being successful in school
- 68% Becoming excited about reading
- 59% Spending time away from technology
- 54% Discovering things he/she might not experience firsthand
- 48% Having time to relax
- 44% Learning from inspiring characters
- 34% Learning ways to deal with experiences he/she is going through
- 27% Being able to forget about real life for a while
- 1% None of these

CHART D

While almost all students enter school longing to learn to read, too many—and any number is too many—leave school disliking reading. When we look at how the number of readers declines between ages six and seventeen, we are dismayed. Additionally, as the information below shows, the number of students who enjoy reading has steadily decreased from 2010 to 2015.

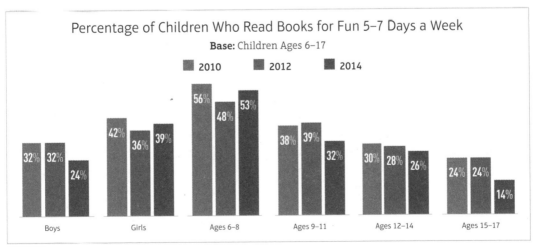

Percentage of Children Who Read Books for Fun 5–7 Days a Week

Base: Children Ages 6–17

2010   2012   2014

	2010	2012	2014
Boys	32%	32%	24%
Girls	42%	36%	39%
Ages 6–8	56%	48%	53%
Ages 9–11	38%	39%	32%
Ages 12–14	30%	28%	26%
Ages 15–17	24%	24%	14%

CHART E

Some would argue video games and online distractions are why kids turn away from reading; others attribute it to the failure of parents to model reading; many blame the overstructured lives of kids, especially teens, in which there is simply no time to read; some say it is the skill-driven environment of schools. The list of contributing factors is a long one. We suspect that all of those factors contribute to the problem and will remain issues for us to confront.

But we also suspect that if we help kids understand that they might read for a more significant purpose than to simply extract information in preparation for a test, then we might make some progress in combating the forces that would yield nonreaders or, perhaps worse, irresponsible readers. If we convince students that reading might sharpen our thinking *and* clarify our emotions, they might see the significant impact it could have on them. In short, we want them to ask themselves, "How has this text changed me?"

Change All the Time?

Bob: I read *The Life-Changing Magic of Tidying Up.*

Kylene: How was it?

Bob: Didn't work. Office is still a mess.

Kylene: Did you follow the advice?

Bob: I read the damned book. Wasn't that enough?

We should be honest: we don't always read to be changed. We don't always go to a text to become something new, wanting to be transformed, to become something else. We don't pick up a book thinking, "I'll read this to change myself" unless the title promises some sort of change we want: *Ten Ways to Get Organized Without Having to Clean Out a Single Closet* or *How to Change Your Eating Habits Without Giving Up Your Favorite Foods.* No, most of the time we go to a text because we want to learn a little, laugh a little, see if we can figure out whodunnit, imagine surviving in a postapocalyptic world. We read to be entertained.

We love that feeling of just letting go, of losing ourselves to the text. That moment in reading when we stand on the bow of the ship with Jacques Cousteau and peer into the deep ocean, when for that moment we are no longer home, on dry land, far away from the ocean, but we are *there*, with the sun on our face and the cold ocean spray stinging our legs, we have lost ourselves to the story, to the experience.

When we close the book, there may be that brief time of looking around, somewhat off-kilter because where we've been and where we are, we realize, have not been the same. There is dinner to be made, papers to be graded, laundry to be washed. Oh well, perhaps we'll just read a bit longer. Losing ourselves in a book is a wonderful experience.

But the most important reading we do is reading that is more than merely pleasurable. It does more than offer moments for us to *lose* ourselves. Indeed, the most important reading we do gives us the chance to *find* ourselves, perhaps to change ourselves. We should at the very least be open to that possibility.

Reading to Be Changed

When we do more than recognize Katniss's compassion, and ask ourselves how her compassion might change our actions; when we do more than ache at Esperanza's loss, and ask ourselves how what we felt will change us; when we do more than cheer Luke on as he bravely decides to come out of hiding, and ask ourselves if we have helped or hindered those who, like Luke, feel they must hide, then we discover something about ourselves and perhaps others.

The reading experience becomes a catalyst for change in our lives. And once you have found that reading can change you, can change how you see the world, can change how you view yourself, then you are more likely to turn to reading again and again, anticipating the possibility that the book will give you some new idea, some new perspective, some new vision that may change who you are slightly or dramatically.

We argue that the ultimate goal of reading is to become more than we are at the moment; to become better than we are now; to become what we did not even know we wanted to become. The transactions we have with texts might enable us to do that. If we read actively, assertively, thoughtfully, responsibly, then any text we read may offer us the possibility that we can reshape ourselves.

We're highlighting some of our favorite characters from *The Hunger Games*, *Esperanza Rising*, and *Among the Hidden*.

We want them to realize that reading should involve disrupting their thinking, changing their understandings of the world and themselves.

The student in the foreground told Kylene, "Come back later. I'm really figuring this out."

Teaching Kids to Expect Change

But in order to read to change, the reader must be responsive to the thoughts and feelings awakened by the text, responsible to both himself and the text, and compassionate and open to the characters and people he finds in the pages, their experiences and ideas, and the reactions of other readers. Our students, however, too often go to reading expecting a grade, not growth. So, we want to disrupt the thinking kids are doing as they read, thinking that is primarily focused on helping them extract evidence from a text. We want them aware of the possibility that reading may—perhaps should—give them the opportunity to reshape themselves.

We want them to realize that reading should involve changing their understandings of the world and themselves. Disrupting thinking should make them want to do more than extract from a text. This is thinking that is characterized by deep intellectual and emotional engagement with the text and themselves. It is thinking that causes them to view themselves and the world, when warranted, in a new light. It is thinking that is generous and yet skeptical; compassionate and yet critical. We want to ask students to be open to the possibility that a text might be disruptive, and that it is that disruption that gives them the opportunity to learn and grow. Reading should be disruptive.

Turn and Talk

Take Two: Chapter 5
scholastic.com/
BeersandProbst

- We believe that if we can encourage kids to read from the head and heart, they will be more likely to read more responsibly what's in the book. Do you agree?

- Think of a text you read that changed something about you. Did you realize it then or later? How important is that text to you?

- What conversations do you have with your students to encourage them to think not only about evidence from the text but how that text is important to them?

Chapter 6

Book, Head, Heart (BHH) Framework

OUR EXPERIMENT with getting kids to read with the possibility of change in mind, willing to let the text be disruptive, got off to a rocky start . . .

We visited one classroom and said to the fifth graders, "As you read, we want you to think about the textual, intellectual, and emotional aspects of the text. In other words, we want you to read responsively and responsibly." We won't even record here how poorly that lesson went.

Next classroom: "Reading can change you. It can open up the world for you. But as you read, you need to think about your responses *and* you need to think about what's in the text. And you ought to ask yourself how this will help you be a compassionate person." One student responded, "Will you two be here *all* week?"

Another day. Another class: "As you read today, we want you to think about what's in the text and at the same time think about what your responses are to what's in the text." The response from the girl on the third row, middle seat: "Did you say if this was for a grade?"

Finally: "Okay. Today, as you read, think about what's in the book, what's in your head, and what's in your heart." Kids looked up. No one said anything. We took that as a good sign and wrote three words on the board: Book. Head. Heart. One boy repeated, "Book. Head. Heart." Another said, "Like what for the head?" We said, "Just ask yourself, 'What surprised me?' Then you'll be thinking about what was in the book while thinking about what you already know." He nodded and said, "Cool." Another asked, "What's a heart question?" We said, "Try 'What did this show me about me?' or 'How could this change how I feel?'" More nods. We held our breath.

The room was quiet. Kids studied our three words as we added some prompts. Then they shrugged and said, "Okay." And there it was. Three words. Book. Head. Heart. Our frame to remind kids that they need to do more than simply extract information from the text.

Parts of the Framework

What do we mean by Book, Head, and Heart? This is simply a short, telegraphic phrase to suggest that we need to pay attention to the text, to our thoughts about it, and to what we feel and how we might have changed, no matter how slightly, as a result of reading. We found that asking fifth graders to attend to the textual, intellectual, and emotional aspects of their reading yielded only blank expressions and glazed-over eyes. (We got the same reaction from their teacher, too.) What did resonate with kids were those three words: *Book*, *Head*, and *Heart*.

It's simple. Direct. And it keeps kids focused on where they must begin—with what's in the book—and where they must end—with how it's changing them. We tell kids, "Of course you must read what's in the book. The author put those words there for a reason! But you also must read thinking about what's in your own head, your responses. And finally you must read thinking about what you took to heart—your feelings, commitments, and values."

BHH Reading

WHEN YOU READ, THINK ABOUT WHAT IS...

• IN THE **BOOK**
  – What's this about?
  – Who's telling the story?
  – What does the author want me to know?

• IN YOUR **HEAD**
  – What surprised me?
  – What does the author think I already know?
  – What changed, challenged or confirmed my thinking?
  – What did I notice?

• IN YOUR **HEART**
  – What did I learn about me?
  – How will this help me to be better?

In the Book

Much of the time we spend in classrooms is devoted to helping kids understand what's in the book. Many writers have helped the profession understand how to help kids think about what's in the text. We often turn to Ellin Keene, Laura Robb, Gay Su Pinnell, Irene Fountas, Kelly Gallagher, Doug Fisher and Nancy Frey, Rozlyn Linder, and Jeff Anderson. We think learning to pay attention to what's in the text is necessary.

Bob: Kylene's first book, *When Kids Can't Read/What Teachers Can Do*, was exclusively about helping kids read what's in the book.

The Common Core State Standards (or your state's current name for these standards) doubles down on focusing on what's in the book. At the 2016 Kentucky Reading Association annual conference, a teacher told us that unless she can prove that the question she is asking is a text-dependent question, she can't ask it. While we think that exclusive focus on the text is not called for, we do want kids to read the text accurately, or as we argued previously, responsibly.

We want students to have strategies to help them notice the author's craft, summarize what they've read, and think about the theme. We know you have your favorite strategies to help students think carefully about what's in the book. Here are a few of our favorite ones.

The Notice and Note Signposts

The Notice and Note Signposts most certainly ask kids to pay attention to what's in the book. We identified critical signposts for students to be alert for in our books *Notice and Note: Strategies for Close Reading* and *Reading Nonfiction: Stances, Signposts, and Strategies*. You can read brief overviews of these in our online resources.

Somebody Wanted But So

When we teach kids how to write a Somebody Wanted But So (Beers, 2003) statement—a single sentence summary statement—we are again helping them focus on the book. This has always been a favorite strategy of ours.

SIGNPOSTS FOR FICTION	
SIGNPOSTS	**DEFINITIONS**
Contrasts and Contradictions	A sharp contrast between what we would expect and what we observe the character doing: behavior that contradicts previous behavior or well-established patterns.
Aha Moment	A character's realization of something that shifts his actions or understanding of himself, others, or the world around him.
Tough Questions	Questions a character raises that reveal his or her inner struggles.
Words of the Wiser	The advice or insight a wiser character, who is usually older, offers about life to the main character.
Again and Again	Events, images, or particular words that recur over a portion of the novel.
Memory Moment	A recollection by a character that interrupts the forward progress of the story.

Somebody Wanted But So

SWBS 🔦 Summarize

Somebody
Peggy Ann McKay...

Somebody is the character

Wanted
...to stay home from school

Wanted is what happened

But
...she has to convince her parents she is sick...

But is the problem

So
...she lies about different diseases until she realizes it's Saturday and she goes to play.

So is the conclusion

See page 89 for the Nonfiction signposts bookmark.

Genre Reformulation

We can also teach them Genre Reformulation (Beers, 2003; Beers & Probst, 2016) and they can reformulate a text into an ABC poster or book as they share information they have learned. Students choose important words or phrases that begin with each letter of the alphabet and represent ideas from the text they've read when making an ABC chart.

Sketch to Stretch

This sixth grader is using Sketch to Stretch (Harste & Burke, 1988; Beers, 2003) to represent visually a powerful line from *Henry's Freedom Box*. As he visually represented his thinking about a particular line, he stretched his understanding of the text. When students sketch what a text represents to them, it helps them focus on specific words, especially important when reading nonfiction.

Fix-Up Charts

When students are confused about something in the text, they often put the book down and look up at the teacher, waiting for her to explain away their confusion. We want teachers to instead point students to fix-up strategy charts so that they, on their own, clarify their confusions.

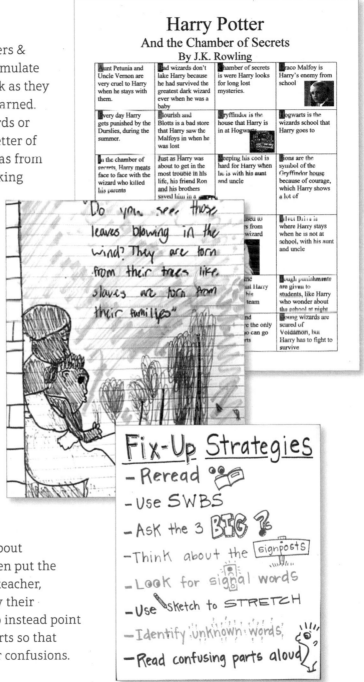

In Your Head

Responsiveness requires that the reader think beyond the four corners of the page; it does not, however, mean dismissing what's on the page. We've both turned to the work of Linda Rief—especially her important text *Read Write Think*—to help us understand more about helping students articulate their own responses to a text. Alfred Tatum, Louise Rosenblatt, Nancie Atwell, Thomas Newkirk, Donald Graves, Stephanie Harvey, and Anne Goudvis also help us all learn more about the responsive nature of reading.

While we want students to understand the text itself, we also want them to see how the text strikes them, and how what it says fits with their own thinking. We want them to reflect on what they are finding in the text. To focus on this intersection of reader and text, we encourage students to consider questions such as:

- What surprised you?
- What did the author think you already knew?
- What changed, challenged, or confirmed your thinking?

This came easily for the students of Heidi Weber, an elementary teacher in Loveland, Ohio. She had already shared the Three Big Questions with her students using sketch notes she created for them.

Her students then made their own bookmarks to use as they were reading.

They easily realized that the "What's in Your Head" thinking was related to the Three Big Questions. When students discuss these questions, they must be thinking about the text and about themselves. It's impossible to talk about what is surprising in a text without having read it and without comparing what it offers to what you already know. As one student said when reading about earthquakes, "I was surprised that it said earthquakes can happen in the ocean. I just thought they had to happen on the ground, you know, on the earth. That really surprised me and now I want to know how that happens." This attention to both the text and your own thoughts and preconceptions, what you have brought to the text, is what makes the reading personal and what enables you to make sense of the reading.

We also want students thinking about how what's in the text connects with other texts they've read, other memories they have, and events going on in the world that the text calls to mind. It was probably Stephanie Harvey and Anne Goudvis's work that helped many of us remind kids that when they read they certainly should make text-to-self, text-to-text, and text-to-world connections. With the publication of their book *Strategies That Work*, we all began to see anchor charts emerge across the nation reminding kids of that important connection and others.

When we began teaching kids to be alert to the signposts they notice in a text, we realized that focusing on a Memory Moment is akin to remembering all the ways a text reminds the reader of other texts, other conversations, other events in his own life, and really harkens to the smart work of Steph and Anne. We encourage you to remind students that the Memory Moments they notice a character having might encourage them to pause and consider their own memories.

Alessandra's bookmark

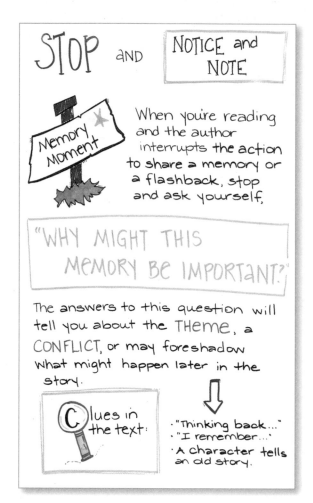

This anchor chart, made by elementary teacher Megan Clappin, helps her students keep this signpost in mind as they read. We would encourage you to remind your students that as they think about what's in their head, they ought to consider what memories this text calls to mind.

In Your Heart

Most certainly, Lester Laminack and Reba Wadsworth's *Bullying Hurts: Teaching Kindness Through Read Alouds and Guided Conversations*, Georgia Heard's *Heart Maps: Helping Students Create and Craft Authentic Writing*, Penny Kittle's *Book Love*, Jeffrey Wilhelm and Michael Smith's *Reading Unbound*, and Pam Allyn and Ernest Morrell's *Every Child a Super Reader* helped us think about this section.

This third element is hardest to define—for us—though kids seem to latch on to it quickly. If "in the head" pointed to the thoughts awakened during the reading—the questions, surprises, unanticipated new information, challenges to assumptions—"in the heart" refers more to the feelings aroused by a text. These feelings are so strong, they move to your heart so you don't let go of them. We've found that it might be easier to talk with students about "what you take to heart" than the more direct "what's in your heart." We think you should use the language that works for your students.

Thinking and feeling are, of course, not easily separated. But there is more to it than emotion alone. "In the heart"—what you take to heart—also refers to the student's sense of self, his values, attitudes, beliefs, and commitments. Those elements are, we think, more than just intellectual, just in the head. In a sense, they involve the whole person and require that our ideas and feelings find their way into our actions, perhaps change who we are.

Taking things to heart—being willing to change, being willing to explore options, listening attentively to yourself and to the text—is not a given. But perhaps we come closer to encouraging some to do just that if we actually spend some time in school valuing statements that show we ourselves are taking students' thinking to heart.

So, we use "in the heart" or "taking to heart" as a way of suggesting that reading is about growing, about changing who we are, about helping us see ourselves in the world from a slightly different perspective. We ask kids:

- What did this text help me learn about myself?
- What did this text help me learn about others?
- How has this text changed my thinking about the world?
- How will my actions or feeling change as a result of reading this text?
- Does this text offer me any of my own Aha Moments? Any Tough Questions? Perhaps my own Words of the Wiser?

After reading *Last Stop on Market Street* by Matt de la Peña, fifth graders discussed the Notice and Note Signposts they noticed in the book. Then they discussed whether or not the book evoked any Aha Moments, Tough Questions, or Words of the Wiser for themselves. Some wrote and some drew their responses. Here is Gabriela's.

All Together

When we introduce BHH to students, we show them the chart and tell them that when we read, we of course need to pay attention to what's in the book. The author put those words there for a reason, so we have to pay attention to what the author is telling us. But we also need to think about what those words mean to us. That's when we're thinking about the ideas the book gives us. And we want to think about how the book makes us feel. We want to think about the lessons we've learned and how we might change as a result of reading the text.

Don't worry if you find yourself confused about whether something is "in the book" or "in your head" or "in your heart." They obviously overlap. Just make sure your readers read beyond the words on the page.

BHH and Social Activism

A teacher asked if our ultimate goal was to turn all our students into social activists. What an interesting question. We've often said we want all students to become productive participants in their community, and we've said that we believe our democracy requires responsive and responsible reading from all of us. Does this mean we're trying to create social activists? If that means being willing to help solve society's problems, yes.

Sometimes the problem is in your own neighborhood as you and neighbors wonder how to help take care of that elderly couple at the end of the street. Perhaps the problem is how to make sure new kids at school don't feel lonely. Perhaps that social problem shows up in your place of worship or your scout troop or your local library. Maybe you become interested in the Society for the Prevention of Cruelty to Animals or one of the walks to help cure cancer or one of the groups that helps build shelters for the homeless. Perhaps you feel called to help build bicycles for underprivileged children or feed the hungry at Thanksgiving or you bring coats to your school for children who, during the winter, would otherwise be cold. Social activism doesn't have to mean heading to Washington to participate in a march about valuing women, but when Kylene's daughter did just that, we found ourselves cheering her on.

If our definition of social activism can be simply to help our society be better, then yes, that's one of our goals for what we think should happen in school. We think raising up those who need help is far more important than raising a test score. We think creating this more compassionate, civic-minded person begins with the texts we have them read and the thinking we ask them to do about those texts.

Book. Head. Heart. Three words. Use them as a frame for talking. A frame for writing. A frame for your own planning. But mostly use them as a way of reminding yourself and your students that we read to do more than learn from the text; we read to do more than enjoy the text. We read to learn more about ourselves. We read to become more than we knew we wanted to be.

Turn and Talk

- What are your thoughts about the BHH framework? How could you use it as a planning tool for yourself and a reading frame for students?

- Do you have students who get stuck in "well, it's my opinion" and refuse to budge? How does this framework help you talk logically with this student?

- Do you and your colleagues discuss social activism? Is volunteering an encouraged effort at your school—for faculty or students?

- Do you think it's important for students to think about how a text is changing them? Do you share with students how reading changes you?

Take Two: Chapter 6
scholastic.com/
BeersandProbst

PART II

Chapter 7

Using the Framework in Your Own Reading

THE BEST WAY to see how the BHH framework can change your own reading is to give it a try.

We want you to read the following poem, "The Journey" by Mary Oliver. As you do, be aware of what's in the book (in this case the "book" is a poem), what's in your head, and what you take to heart. You might do this the way we do—read it through one time, just taking in the whole poem. Then read it a second time, this time taking note of those three aspects.

To think about what's in the book, focus on whatever it is that catches your attention. Simply read, asking yourself, "What's going on in this text? What do I notice in it? What does the author want me to know?" Next, to think about what's in your head, focus on one big question: "What surprised me?" Finally, to think about what's in your heart, ask, "What did I learn about myself?" or "How will this change me?"

We can't tell you where to begin—book, head, or heart. Each reader is different. But we do encourage you to reflect on all three areas. Other times, with other texts, you might find yourself focused more on what's in your heart than what's in the text, but this one time, humor us. Try to attend to all three.

Read and Reflect

The Journey

One day you finally knew
what you had to do, and began,
though the voices around you
kept shouting
their bad advice—
though the whole house
began to tremble
and you felt the old tug
at your ankles.
"Mend my life!"
Each voice cried.
But you didn't stop.
You knew what you had to do,
though the wind pried
with its stiff fingers
at the very foundations—
though their melancholy
was terrible.

It was already late
enough, and a wild night,
and the road full of fallen
branches and stones.
But little by little,
as you left their voices behind,
the stars began to burn
through the sheets of clouds,
and there was a new voice,
which you slowly
recognized as your own,
that kept you company
as you strode deeper and deeper
into the world,
determined to do
the only thing you could do—
determined to save
the only life you could save.

—Mary Oliver. "The Journey," in *Dream Work*, New York, NY: Atlantic Monthly Press, 1986, p. 38.

This is a poem for adults, because even as folks who love children's and young adult literature, we find from time to time that it is enjoyable to read something written for an adult!

PART II

Our Conversation

Bob and I did exactly what we've just asked you to do: we read the poem and then discussed it in writing via Skype using the BHH frame and some of the signposts and big questions.

 [10:51:49 AM] KyleneBeers: You want to start with what you noticed in the book—meaning "The Journey"?

 [10:56:20 AM] Robert E. Probst: Yes, and what struck me in the text was the phrase "there was a new voice, which you slowly recognized as your own"—the idea of slowly recognizing your own voice was startling. I'd think that your own voice would be one you'd recognize immediately. So there's something in "voice" that's more than just characteristic sounds and rhythms.

 [10:59:44 AM] KyleneBeers: You know, while you were typing, I realized that even though I asked you if you wanted to start with what's in the book, I had really gone first to what was in my heart. From the beginning, there was something about this that spoke to my heart. Maybe it's because it's titled "The Journey" and right now with this book, it feels like we're on such a journey. But that first thought took me immediately back to the text. I think I do that too often with kids—being in the book feels safer, so I start them there—even when I KNOW I'll get the more honest and probably much deeper response if I start them either in their head or their heart.

And as I look at what you wrote, I'm struck that what you saw was a Contrast and Contradiction. You're right—you would think that you would recognize your own voice. Unless you've been in a situation where your voice hasn't been respected. Hasn't been heard—not even by yourself.

[11:07:12 AM] Robert E. Probst: Or where you haven't heard your own voice because it's been drowned out in the noise of others. "Hearing your own voice" suggests to me "understanding yourself," and sometimes that isn't easy to do because you accept roles and expectations of others. It was expected that I'd go to college, but looking back I don't know if that was my own "voice" or not—maybe I was just doing what everyone expected. At one point, I thought I'd like to spend my life as a professional diver, but by then I was in another life, as professor, husband, father, someone with bills to pay. I don't know whether I ignored what my own voice was telling me, or if I suppressed it, or it was just idle daydreaming. I suspect it's hard to identify your own voice sometimes.

[11:12:09 AM] KyleneBeers: You know, that was one of the things that surprised me as I read this—that the narrator was hearing other voices just fine—so clear the narrator could even quote what they were saying, "Mend my life," but could barely recognize her own voice. And I'm saying "her" on purpose because I see the narrator as female. What surprised me was that it seems the journey—which sounds like an actual trip—might have really been a journey to finding her own voice. That made me think that the most important journeys we take are within ourselves, discoveries of ourselves. What did you think of as you were taking things to heart?

[11:15:34 AM] Robert E. Probst: I think I realized that I have to spend more time inside myself. I have to go stare at the water and try to silence all the other voices that tell me what to do or whom to be. Maybe I need to learn to meditate. I suspect that I should put some moments of solitude into each day, just so that I can try to hear my own voice a little more clearly. Whether I'll recognize it or not, if I do hear it, is another question!

[11:19:08 AM] KyleneBeers: That's what you were taking to heart—that you need to give yourself the chance to sit quietly to actually hear your own voice. That's probably an important lesson for me, too. Interesting, we started with a look at how the narrator didn't recognize her own voice and ended up recognizing that in our own lives we might not give ourselves the time and space to do the same. Nice, Dr. Probst.

As you can imagine, with more time and more people, the conversation might have gone on much longer, and might have roamed over many more and different reflections. You might notice, too, that although we ended up talking about ourselves, we never strayed far from the text and were always inclined to go back to it. And we noticed that our talk gave us ideas for things we both wanted to write. It reminded each of us of memories that might serve as the focus of poems of our own, or, perhaps just a few reflective paragraphs. If we want to write about the text, the poem gave us some specifics such as that interesting line about recognizing your own voice.

Most important, though, our conversation made the text important to us, gave it a place in our lives, helped us think about matters that were of significance to us. We weren't just answering the teacher's questions, or the questions at the end of the selection in the textbook. We were creating and exploring our own questions. If students have similar experiences with texts on a regular basis, they are more likely, we believe, to realize that reading can be significant, and that it can help them shape their perceptions of themselves and their place in the world.

Consider repeating this exercise under different circumstances. As we've just done, first, take a poem (or a short article, essay, or editorial) that you found interesting, and in solitude give some thought to these three elements:

- What you noticed in the text
- What happened in you, your thinking, as you read the text

- What you took to heart, what touched you or made you look at yourself or your world in a new way

Then do this with a partner, as we did. Either sit down together in a quiet room over a cup of coffee and talk, or do it as a Skype conversation, typing in your thoughts. The advantage of doing it that way is that it will give you a record of your conversation that you can return to later. Next, and perhaps with another text, do this with a larger group. The more you read with this framework in mind, the more you learn about how reading can shape your own thinking, and the easier it will be to convey to your students how reading can shape *their* thinking.

So, of course, try it out with your students. Experiment with different structures, different group sizes, different texts, and be patient with yourself, your kids, and the process. Either audio- or video-record one or two of the student conversations so that you can assess them at your leisure. In the next chapter, we share some student conversations we've captured.

Turn and Talk

We've shared our written Skype conversation here so you can see how the prompts inspired by the BHH framework helped to move us along. You might try having a written conversation with a colleague. In a college classroom reading this poem, one student said, "This is so much better than reading and just answering the questions from the back of our book." What did you think? Did reading with the BHH framework in mind change your thinking? Sharpen it in any way? We used a poem because we think that poetry, more than other genres, ought to speak to the heart. When you first introduce this frame to students, you might consider introducing it through poems. If you were to use a poem with younger students, we suggest trying something by Shel Silverstein such as "The Little Boy and the Old Man." The narrative structure of most of his poems will be helpful.

Take Two: Chapter 7
scholastic.com/
BeersandProbst

PART II

Chapter 8

Using the Framework in the Classroom

IN THIS CHAPTER, we share four examples of how BHH helped students think through a text. We begin by entering a first-grade classroom.

First Grade

The first graders laughed loudly, rolling on the floor, as their teacher finished reading *The Book with No Pictures* by B. J. Novak. After the last page, the teacher let the students enjoy talking about it with each other before trying to restore calm. Then she pointed them to the BHH chart she had up in the room and asked them to turn to a partner and talk about something that mattered to them.

Student 1: I loved loved loved this story!

Student 2: It was so funny. Does that make it in the book or in my head?

Student 1: It is in the heart for me because I loved it so much.

Student 2: But you loved it because of what was in the book.

Student 1: But it was my heart that loved it.

Student 2: Maybe it was in your head. Because you have to think about loving it. But it is also in your heart. But it had to start in the book. They are like all smooshed together.

Student 1: Nope. It's in my heart. I love love love it.

Student 2: But can it be in more than one place?

What We Noticed

We applaud Student 2. She understood that response is "all smooshed together." Though the anchor chart shows book, head, and heart as separate aspects of reading, the reality is that they are interdependent. What's in the book affects your thinking; and your more critical thinking certainly affects your emotional, affective response. It will sometimes be helpful to remind students to go back into the book for evidence or clarification; it will sometimes be helpful to ask them what they can infer or what they wonder about or what surprised them—all "in my head" thinking; and it will sometimes be most valuable to spend time considering how the text has changed their understanding of themselves and others—"in my heart" thinking. But response, true response, is (to borrow the wisdom of a first grader) all smooshed together.

Fourth Grade

The fourth-grade students sat on the floor around their teacher's rocking chair as she read aloud a picture book to them. Once they finished this daily routine, she directed their attention to the BHH anchor chart that they had been discussing for several weeks. She reminded them, "As you read, remember the goal is for you to be a BHH reader. You've got to pay attention to what's in the book because that's

what the author chose to tell you or what the illustrator chose to show you. Right?" Eagerly, heads nodded.

She continued, "But you also need to pay attention to what's in your head because your own experiences will help you make sense of what the author is telling you." She paused because Adam was wildly waving his hand. He added, "So that's where you have to ask yourself 'What surprised me?' because then you are really thinking about what the author is saying to *you*."

The teacher agreed with Adam and added, "You can also just keep asking yourself, 'What's this making me think about now?'" Students nodded. Then she finished her reminder: "And finally, pay attention to what you take to heart. This might help you understand how the text might change you." Now other students were waving their hands. The teacher called on Ana Sofia first.

Ana Sofia: When we read *Too Many Tamales*, it was like my heart-reading for me was most important because I kept asking myself my own Tough Questions, you know, what would I do? It was like I was thinking about Maria and me at the same time.

Orlando: Miss, this was hard at first because all we had been doing until last year was thinking, "Is it evidence?" But when you said, "Think about times you had an aha," then I really like it because it is like you notice the character's Aha Moment and get to think about your own ahas and that is better. Like with *A Handful of Stars*, I didn't want to read it at first, because it looked like a girl book but then I liked it because it had the migrant workers and my cousins are migrant workers and suddenly I was having aha after aha. Like I was thinking how it must feel to have to move all the time. That made me think I should be more aware of their feelings. I like reading BHH best because it is what makes reading have a lot of meaningful to you."

The teacher gently helped Orlando restate his last sentence, but there is something we like about his wording. When a book finds its way from the page to your head to your heart, we suspect it does indeed have "a lot of meaningful to you."

Teacher: Okay. Head on back to your seats. I'll be meeting with Group 3 first today, so if your name is up here as a part of Group 3, go ahead and get your books and meet me at the table. The rest of you should be reading on your own. I want you to enjoy what you're reading, so only stop to reflect on these BHH prompts if a thought pops into your head or when you find a logical place to pause. Then jot down in your journal things you don't want to forget— what you noticed about what's in the book, what's in your head, or what's in your heart. Or wait until you've finished reading and make notes then.

What We Noticed

We like that this teacher had followed through on our thought that the literary signposts that we've taught students could now be used to help them think about their own responses. We also thought it was important for the teacher to tell the students to read for enjoyment first. Enjoy the journey! But if something occurs to you and you don't want to lose it, pause and jot it down. We think she has a very common-sense approach to finding the balance between reading and thinking about what you are reading.

Eighth Grade

The small group of eighth-grade students from New York City—five boys and one girl—met with their teacher for an end-of-day class designed to help students who potentially will not score well on their state test. Their teacher agreed to try the BHH framework as group members read a short nonfiction article, "Garana's Story: A Day in the Life of a Young Afghan Refugee."

The students and their teacher sat clustered at a small table. She put the BHH anchor chart in the center, turned on a recorder, then read "Garana" aloud as students followed along, and captured this conversation afterward.

Teacher: What do you want to talk about first: in the book, in the head, or in the heart?

Boy 1: I think in the head. Because I was surprised.

Teacher: What surprised you?

Boy 1: That she lived in that one-room house for all that time. I didn't know they had to live like that for so long.

Boy 2: That's what I would say, too.

Boy 3: Well, like they had to move from one house to another and . . .

Boy 4: Oh, I know what you mean. When the bombings . . . They had to move . . .

Boy 3: They had to flee. I can't imagine someone bombing New York City and we had to leave because of that.

Boy 6: There was something in China where they had a bomb and when the bomb hit there was something called toxic rain and when the bomb hit they started to die.

Boy 3: Allāhu Akbar. Allāhu Akbar. That's what she would have to say at the mosque. Allāhu Akbar.

Boy 4: How do you know that?

Boy 3: Because it is on TV. Allāhu Akbar. It means something about God.

Teacher: It means "God is great."

Boy 5: So she wears one of those things on her head.

Boy 3: Yeah. What's it called?

Teacher: Hijab.

Boy 5: Yeah she wears a hijab.

Teacher: [To the girl] What's something that surprised you?

Girl: That they were so poor. Like really poor. Here in the U.S., well at least in New York City, if you need something, you can just go get it. You aren't that poor.

Boy 2: Some people are. They don't even have one of those camps. They just sleep in streets.

Boy 1: I have a heart thing.

Teacher: Okay.

Boy 1: This made me very, I don't know, it made my heart think how I didn't know there were people who were that poor. I thought they just wore their scarves and went around saying Allahu Akbar but this little girl, she's just like our age, and she has to do all this stuff and her dad is gone. I was thinking you know here [pointing to the anchor chart] where it says "How will this change you?" It's going to make me more, like considerate. Like just because you look different, you might not really be all that different. Man, like I'm going to have to really think about that.

Teacher: Which of these did you like best: book, head, or heart?

Boy 1: For me, heart. Because we never talk about this at school. Like Afghanistan. You just hear about it on the news, but we haven't ever really talked about what does this mean to us at school.

Boy 3: I wish we did this more.

Boy 2: This made it, when you really think about how they live, when *you* think about it, then it is different. I like it from the heart.

What We Noticed

We eliminated some of the chatter that happens in small-group conversations at the end of a long school day: "Do you think it will snow tonight?" "Do macadamia nut cookies have macadamia nuts in them?" "I think my mom said I have to leave early." We thought the teacher was a saint for staying calm. We are positive she—all of you—deserve a raise. Now. Simply for showing up.

What we notice most about this conversation is the wide range of information these children bring to the table: an Arab phrase they had heard, knowledge of the clothing the women wear, a bombing in China, an awareness that the poverty that Garana and her family faced was different from the poverty they see in New York City. We know this school and can imagine the poverty endured by many of the children sitting in this classroom. And yet, they still saw Garana as the poor one. But for us, the part of this conversation that made us fall in love with middle schoolers all over again was the admission from a couple of the boys that what they miss at school is conversations about how texts touch their hearts. "I like it from the heart." We think there's a valuable lesson there for us all to remember.

College Freshman

Kylene: My neighbor's daughter is a freshman at a university not too far from where I live. She was home for a weekend and, surprise, I was too! Her mom called me and asked if Jodi could come over for some help. Seems she was struggling with the reading in one of her classes.

She arrived quickly and explained that in one class, each student had to prepare a two-minute summary of the assigned reading. Each time she had shared a summary, her professor told that her it sounded as if it were "for an elementary school class" or "just a retell" or "not college level at all." When Jodi would ask her professor for help, he would tell her that she needed to be "more academic," but beyond that, Jodi found his comments vague and not helpful.

Jodi was an A student in her very academic public high school. She was in AP English and made a 4 on the AP test. She said, "I don't know what he wants from me. In high school, all we had to do was answer the questions and as long as we gave evidence from the text, we were okay. Now, the rules have shifted but no one has told me what they are."

　　She was in tears. Her roommate wasn't working out; the community bathroom was a struggle; the food on campus was okay but not great; she wasn't making a lot of friends; her parents didn't want her to join a sorority but that seemed the only way to be in a group; she missed her brother. We forget—I think—that the excitement of *going away to* college soon turns to the reality of *being away at* college. I've known Jodi for a long time. I have enjoyed watching her childhood from the perspective of the neighbor who has shared a glass of wine with her mom as we have both navigated the joys (truly) and frustrations (truly) of raising daughters. I thought about what I could quickly offer this kid who looked more like a scared adolescent than a college student.

Me:　　Jodi, I want to show you something that Bob and I are trying right now with kids to help them with reading, but I don't see any reason why it won't help you with thinking about a summary for what you've read. Do you have to write these summaries?

Jodi:　　Yes. The professor doesn't call on everyone. If he calls on you, you have to read it. It can't be more than two minutes. Otherwise you turn it in.

Me:　　Okay. So, use this as a writing frame. I don't normally like writing frames, but when you're learning something new, a frame can be extremely helpful.

Jodi:　　Like a writing formula. We did hamburger writing in middle school. I'll take anything.

Me:　　Well, I hope this isn't like hamburger writing because I really dislike that formula. But let's give this a try. First, are you reading the material?

Jodi:　　I am. All of it. I promise.

Me:　　I believe you. What are you doing as you read it?

Jodi:　　I'm underlining everything that seems important. That's hard because in high school, what was important was highlighted for you. Now you have to do it yourself.

Me: So are all your pages yellow? [Jodi laughs and nods.] Do this. As you read, put an exclamation point by what surprises you and then in the margin, jot down why it surprises you. Then if you come across something that you don't know a lot about, and the author doesn't tell you much about it, put a question mark next to it and, in the margin, write whatever question comes to your mind. Finally, if there's a part that causes you to change your mind on something or makes you say to yourself, "I don't think so!" or maybe confirms what you think, then in the margin put the letter C for change, challenge, or confirm. That's what I want you to do as you read.

Jodi: Okay. How does that help me with my summary?

Me: It's helping you think about the text. Next, I want you to keep the BHH reading frame in mind. That stands for Book, Head, and Heart. And that's just a reminder that when you read, you need to think about what's in the book, what's in your head, and what you take to heart. You're going to then use BHH to help you write your summary. You need to write about something in the book, in your head, and in your heart.

Jodi: I like it. BHH.

Me: When you get ready to write your summary, I want you to write a couple of sentences about what the text said. Next, I want you to write a few sentences on what surprised you; or what the author was talking about that you need more information on; or how the text changed your mind.

Jodi: So that's why I'm marking those parts as I read.

Me: Right. Finally, I want you to think about what you took to heart. And that's where I want you to write a couple of sentences about how what you have read has changed how you think. If it hasn't, then perhaps what questions it has raised for you. And if it hasn't done that, then perhaps what else you want to read on this topic.

Jodi: I like it. So first, write about what was in the book, then in my head, then in my heart.

Me: That's it. When is your next one due?

Jodi: Tuesday.

What I Noticed

On Thursday, Jodi called to tell me that her professor told her it was the best two-minute summary he had ever heard. She said that other kids in the class—who were also struggling—wanted to know how she did it. She happily shared the BHH frame.

I know this is a formula. And I know that the best writing is not formulaic. But I also know that when you're learning a new writing genre—and this was very new for her—a frame can help. My son, in law school as I'm writing this, is learning to write briefs. He's learning to write them by doing two things: reading a lot of briefs and being told the formula that a brief must follow. Sometimes a frame helps. Jodi's professor didn't offer her a frame. That's all she needed. Since BHH is a frame for helping students think through a text, there is no reason it couldn't also help kids write about their reading.

Turn and Talk

- What did you see in these classrooms you found interesting or worth exploring with a colleague?

- Do the conversations in your classroom already reflect these three aspects of the reading experience? If not, which aspect needs attention?

- We presented BHH anchor charts on pages 63, 78, and 80 to indicate there are many ways to present this information. Which way would work best for your students?

Take Two: Chapter 8
scholastic.com/
BeersandProbst

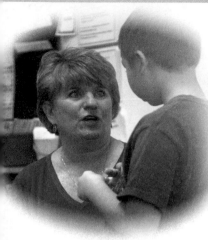

Chapter 9

Big Questions, Signposts, and the BHH Framework

OUR COLLABORATIVE THINKING about literacy issues began many years ago. The central idea for all of our work has remained constant over those years, and it is essentially the vision that Louise Rosenblatt offered the profession. It is the idea that the reader matters, that meaning doesn't reside solely within the text, but that it is made by the reader. In short, the reader must be responsive and responsible. This thinking has evolved, changed by our time in schools working with students and teachers, and in our several books, it has taken slightly differing shapes.

- In the first book, *Notice and Note*, we presented six signposts that readers should stay alert for as they read literary texts. The signposts help readers recognize the author's theme.

- In *Reading Nonfiction*, we shared the Three Big Questions that help readers adopt a questioning stance and we shared five new signposts for nonfiction that help readers understand author's purpose and bias.

- In this book, we're exploring what it means to invite reading to disrupt thinking. Additionally, we want to show how the BHH framework can help you organize your instruction and can help your students realize that reading what's in the book and in their head can help them think about what they want to take to heart.

Asking the Three Big Questions

As students make inferences, they are thinking about what's *in their head*. For our most concrete learners, we've learned that telling them to make an inference can be more confusing than helpful. We've found that we can get kids to make an inference much more easily if we can get them to discuss any of the Three Big Questions that we present in *Reading Nonfiction*:

- What surprised you?
- What did the author think you already knew?
- What changed, challenged, or confirmed your thinking?

While these questions were presented in a book about nonfiction, we've come to see that they are just as valuable for fiction. These in-the-head questions require that students also be thinking about what's in the book. Beware: we discovered the hard way that asking a first grader, "What surprised you?" might mean you never move from page one. We tend to ask our youngest readers, "What surprised you the most?"

See page 37 for an anchor chart of these Big Questions.

Noticing the Signposts

When you teach students the Notice and Note Signposts, you're helping them pay attention to what's in the book. Put another way, you're helping them focus on the author's craft. If you don't plan to teach these signposts, we know there are many other ways you are helping kids think about what's in the book. But if you teach students to notice Extreme and Absolute Language (for example), then you are asking them to stay alert to specific language that's in the book, language that might reveal a bias. Or if you teach them to notice Aha Moments, you are asking them to recognize those places where the character has realized something. That realization will probably change the direction of the plot. Those "in the book" signposts help the

SIGNPOSTS FOR NONFICTION	
SIGNPOSTS	DEFINITIONS
Contrasts and Contradictions	A sharp contrast between what we would expect and what we observe happening. A difference between two or more elements in the text.
Extreme and Absolute Language	Language that leaves no doubt about a situation or an event, allows no compromise, or seems to exaggerate or overstate a case.
Numbers and Stats	Specific quantities or comparisons to depict the amount, size, or scale. Or the writer is vague and imprecise about the numbers when we would expect more precision.
Quoted Words	Words that are quoted are quoted for a reason. They might offer evidence or a personal perspective.
Word Gaps	Vocabulary that is unfamiliar to the reader. This might be because it is a word with multiple meanings, a rare or technical word, a discipline-specific word, or one with a far-removed antecedent.

These are the Nonfiction signposts. The bookmark for the Fiction signposts appeared on page 64.

reader to think about theme (for literary texts) or author's purpose (for nonfiction texts).

What You Take to Heart

It was Eileen Ours, a teacher in Solon, Ohio, who first mentioned to us that when she asked her students to think about what was in their heart they just stared at her. That was not the response we wanted. She then explained that she helped her students think about what they were taking to heart by asking them to think about the signposts, but in a slightly different way. She said to them, "You know that one of the signposts is Aha Moments. That's when the character figures out something that will make a difference in what that character does next. Well, when you are reading and you have your *own* Aha Moment, then that's something you have taken to heart from this book." Her students got it. We did, too. When the reader notices something the character has figured out, that's a signpost in the book. But when the reader has his own Aha Moment, creates his own Tough Questions, has her own Memory Moment, realizes her own Words of the Wiser, then that reader has taken something from the text to heart. We wished we had seen this ourselves.

She offered her students another example. "You know to be alert to places in the text where the character asks a Tough Question. You know that those Tough Questions usually reveal something that makes the character struggle, a worry or problem the character has. Well, when you are reading and something in the book causes a Tough Question inside you, then that's something that you've taken to heart." More nods from her students. Even more from us.

And a final example: "Plus, you know that as you read fiction, at some point an older, wiser character will usually offer some Words of the Wiser to the main character. The words are the smart advice that the main character ought to follow. When you are reading and realize that something from the book has, in a way, offered you advice you want to follow, then your heart has found its own Words of the Wiser."

We thought Eileen had offered her students a smart way to move the signposts from words they noticed in the text to feelings and thoughts they noticed in themselves.

Signposts and Taking the Book to Heart

After third graders read *Hank the Cowdog* and drew pictures in response, Thahn decided to show the heart lesson she had learned by focusing on the Words of the Wiser. She said, "I'm not sure Hank had any Words of the Wiser. He had more Again and Again. But I had a Word of the Wiser." Her comment shown in the picture below said, "You don't have to always think you are better."

In a fifth-grade classroom, the teacher was reading aloud *Roll of Thunder, Hear My Cry* to her students. One day, after finishing another chapter, the teacher asked the students to think about what they were taking to heart by simply asking themselves, "What Tough Questions does this book raise for me?" One student responded:

> "That scene where she wants a new book but the teacher says that's all they get, that makes me wonder about the times we donate things to our church. It goes to people who don't have things. But sometimes I just put away my worst clothes. I hadn't thought that someone was going to look at that and think shouldn't I also have nice things. When I was thinking what are my Tough Questions, I wondered if I should be giving away my better stuff, you know, so that the kid getting them would feel a little more proud."

PART II

An eighth-grade boy shared the piece below in response to *The Watsons Go to Birmingham–1963*. He noticed Contrasts and Contradictions in the text as Byron sometimes acted like a bully and other times acted like someone with a conscience. Then our eighth grader noticed a Contrast and Contradiction within himself:

> I noted a Contrast and Contradiction with Byron because he is always acting so tough but then he doesn't. Like how he was after he killed the bird or how he was after Kenny was so scared. He is like a tough guy but not really. So, when we had to be thinking about heart, I was like thinking at first Aha Moments but then I thought you know it's like now I'm a Contrast and Contradiction because I didn't know much about them bombing churches, you know white people doing that. It made me see that this happened not too far from here. I really feel like I need to know more about this. And that's a contradiction for me because I don't usually like history. I don't know if this makes my heart happy or not.

This student's final line, "I don't know if this makes my heart happy or not," brings up an issue we had not considered. He seems to have internalized that if you are considering something from your heart—how it makes you feel, how it is changing you—the response must be positive. Of course, though, that's not true. In this case, he realizes that he wants to know more about the church bombings of the 1960s during the Civil Rights era, as unhappy as it may make him. Yes, when we change, we are not always happy with what we've discovered.

We close this section with a written comment from one of Eileen's sixth-grade students. This student shares how reading with BHH in mind has changed her reading. We were particularly interested in her final comments as she compares her own response to a book with the response of a friend. She explains that her friend did not know the BHH framework. She concluded that, "I found a lot more meaning to the book than she did and I found more little things that were important later on in the book than she did." We appreciate her student-as-researcher stance.

Not all students appreciate this frame. One third grader reported, "When I read with BHH my head gets all these thoughts I never wanted there."

> I think that it helps me with my Reading Because when I Read B+6 I felt like I UnderStood the Book a lot more then any other Book I have Read Because of BHH Reading Because it has me thinking of everything at once. •What is happing with the Book •What Do I think •What Do I feel. So If I am thinking about all of That then I am going to understand it better and get the hole feeling of The Book. And As we were using This Strat'gere I was trying it on a Book That my friend Read at the Same time. except I used the Strat'ge and She did not and I found a lot more meaning to the Book than She did and I found more little things that were Important later on In the Book then She did So I had a

Turn and Talk

- What strategies do you most often use—other than teacher questions—to help your students think about what's in the book?

- If you're using the signposts with your students, which ones do they tend to notice most often?

- We can't stress enough that BHH is a framework that presents information in a linear fashion, but we can't dictate the order in which someone responds to a text. For instance, we suspect you've heard a tune you love and find yourself calling it a favorite song long before you ever analyze the words. Or you might find yourself emotionally responding to a poem before you ask yourself what caused that response. How can you help your students recognize that BHH is a framework and not a specific order of response?

Take Two: Chapter 9
scholastic.com/
BeersandProbst

PART III
THE CHANGES WE MUST EMBRACE

Opening Comments

LET'S TAKE A LOOK at comments from three students. The first two are from Katie and LaTonya, who scored 3 on their reading comprehension state test (with 4 being the highest); the third is from Eric, who scored in the lowest quartile of his state test.

Katie is a fifth-grade student in an inner-city elementary school of about 800 students. The school is 60 percent Latino, 25 percent African American, and 15 percent white, Asian, or "other." She is well liked and enjoyable to be around. Her teacher explained that while Katie "isn't really a leader, she's not actually a follower" and worries that in middle school "she could be one of those kids who gets overlooked because she doesn't demand too much of your attention."

Kylene: Do you enjoy reading?

Katie: Not really. I mean it can be okay sometime. If the story is really good. But. No. Not too much.

> We noticed the bulletin board in the hallway outside this fifth-grade classroom was filled with drawings of clouds under the caption "We Love Clouds."

Kylene: Why is that?

Katie: I don't know. Like, it's just really boring. Like in science what are the different types of clouds.

Kylene: Your teacher said you're a good reader.

Katie: I guess. I mean I can answer the questions. I get like 85s and 90s. That's pretty good. But the questions aren't hard and then if you draw good pictures, like we had to draw pictures of the different types of clouds and I'm good at drawing, so then you get a 100 and so that was good. So, yeah, I guess I'm a good reader.

Kylene: Can you tell me what you learned about yourself from that article you just read?

Katie: Learned about me? I don't know what you mean.

The following conversation happened in the same school, but with LaTonya, a fourth grader. This child, described by her teacher as "one of those kids who never causes any problems," was, in our eyes, beginning to exhibit frustration about school.

Bob: Do you like to read?

LaTonya: Nope.

Bob: Can you tell me why that is?

LaTonya: It's like, who cares? You read. You answer questions. You get a grade. You read again. You answer questions. You get a grade. I hate it

Bob: Your teacher told us that you are a good reader.

LaTonya: Really? Okay.

The student in this final conversation, Eric, is from a suburban middle school of about 1,100 students that had equal numbers of African American, Latino, and white students. Very few students qualified for free or reduced lunches. Eric is in eighth grade and is making mostly Cs and Ds. He is in a remedial reading class, which he hates. His teacher told us, "I think he's got more potential than his test scores show, but I really don't have evidence for that. He walks in. Slumps into his chair." We were interested in the teacher's hunch that this kid had potential, which his attitude and scores weren't indicating. We asked the teacher if he had explored that hunch by talking with Eric. "Not really. I've tried. But I've got thirty-eight students that period."

Bob: Do you like to read?

Eric: Not too much.

Bob: Why is that?

Eric: It just doesn't matter too much to me. I mean the teacher says read this and answer that. Then you have to be taking tests. If you don't get 90 percent then you don't go on.

Bob: Do you ever read at home?

Eric: Home? Not really. Well, maybe if you count computer stuff.

Bob: What do you read on your computer?

Eric: No, I didn't mean I was reading on a computer. I meant I read things about computers. I'm really interested in what's going to happen with the next search engines. How they're going to do more than just pull information together. It's more like artificial intelligence. That's really interesting.

Bob: Sounds like you do like to read.

Eric: No. Well, not the kind of reading teachers say is important.

Bob: How is the reading you do at home different from what you do at school?

Eric: I don't know. It's like reading at school is to analyze points of view or compare and contrast a song to a story. We had to do that so much last year. The teacher said we needed more rigor. But I just don't care about it. But when I'm home, it's what I picked out. I don't know. Home reading feels different.

Bob listens as a student explains what he likes and doesn't like about reading.

> Reading at school is always, just, different. At home it's like just what I do to figure out something. At school it's just answering questions.

Bob: So, at home you're asking the questions and at school you're *answering* the questions someone else has asked.

Eric: Yeah! That's good. You should write that down.

The act of reading called to mind a specific set of practices for these students: being told what to read and being told what questions to answer about the reading. These practices had so shaped Katie's thinking that she wondered if my question about what was most interesting was an attempt to get her to recount the main idea. LaTonya had turned the process into three steps: 1. read 2. answer 3. get a grade. Eric's thinking about reading was filtered by years of reading to answer questions. He could not reconcile his satisfaction with the home reading experience with his dissatisfaction with the school reading experience. He had taken his literacy underground.

We want to disrupt the thinking of these kids. And we want these kids to welcome the disruption that reading might bring to their thinking.

We want to disrupt the thinking of these kids. And we want these kids to welcome the disruption that reading might bring to their thinking. We want the recording in their heads—read to answer, read to answer, read to answer—to get unstuck so they can move on to more powerful ideas. Disrupting their thinking, though, might require disrupting some of our own thinking about big issues. We explore those issues in this section.

Remember, in the Introduction we pointed out two questions that we need to consider to be open to disruptive thinking: What needs to change? What assumptions need to be challenged? In Part III, we share big issues we think need to change and offer assumptions that might need to be challenged.

Chapter 10

From Now to Next

PRIOR TO 1808, it took a skilled craftsman about six weeks to two months to make one clock, and so production clicked by slowly and yielded only about ten clocks per year.

Each clock, and each piece within each clock, was made entirely by hand by a craftsman—and perhaps his apprentice—who worked laboriously, and we like to think, lovingly, over each part. Each cog, each gear, each spring, each weight, each face and hand—all were handmade. And while this created a clock of fine craftsmanship—one hoped—it was a slow, laborious, and therefore expensive process. Owning a clock was a luxury.

Then in 1808, in that one year alone, Eli Terry, Connecticut clockmaker, produced 3,000 clocks. What allowed him to move from ten clocks in a year to thousands? One idea. Once concept. One disruption to the traditional way of doing business: He figured out how to mass-produce parts that could be interchangeable from one clock to the next. This one idea enabled Terry to mass-produce clocks. This was a decade-long process as he figured out how to take a grain mill and use the water wheel in it to run the saws mechanically. Next, he standardized the size of parts of clocks so that one part could work in any clock. And that was the key. Once parts were generic and interchangeable, then mass production could begin.

In England, at about the same time, Marc Brunel helped lead the production of about 100,000 pulley blocks the Royal Navy needed for its ships. Using interchangeable parts, Brunel was able to scale up production so that fewer men and less time were needed to make this critical component.

Brunel's work built upon the late-18th century work of Honoré Blanc, who looked at how to make interchangeable parts for firearms. Thomas Jefferson, who was then Ambassador to France, saw what Blanc was doing and brought the idea back to the United States. Eli Whitney then applied the idea of interchangeable parts for firearms here in the States, though most historians credit Captain John Hall and Simeon North for successfully applying the concept first.

Suffice it to say, interchangeable parts come to us via a long history—dating all the way back to the First Punic War, 264–241 BCE. If they hadn't arrived, though, the movable assembly line (developed by Henry Ford) wouldn't have worked and the Industrial Revolution wouldn't have happened. That one disruption changed everything.

In education, we don't talk much about disruptive practices, but it is an issue we ought to address. We tend to be more enamored with "best practices." Educators borrowed the concept of best practices from the business and medical communities and hold on to it as though it will solve all our problems. When we want to assure parents, policy makers, and principals that we're doing the right thing, we tell others (and perhaps ourselves) that we're following a best practice. And that sounds good. It's certainly better than saying, "Hey, at our school we follow mostly good practices, one or two fairly good practices, and some practices that are just okay." Yes, it's easy to see why *best practice* is a popular term.

It's such a popular term that it is almost meaningless. In October 2016, when we turned to Google and entered "best practices in education," we had 330,000 hits (in .37 seconds). We decided not to read them all, but these three definitions will give you a sense of the range of definitions/descriptions we found as we looked through several (meaning not 333,000) articles:

- "Existing practices that already possess a high level of widely agreed effectiveness" (Hargreaves & Fullan, 2012).
- "The wide range of individual activities, policies, and programmatic approaches to achieve positive changes in student attitudes or academic behaviors" (EOA National Best Practices Center, 2016).

- "Best practices are an inherent part of a curriculum that exemplifies the connection and relevance identified in educational research. They inject rigor into the curriculum by developing thinking and problem-solving skills through integration and active learning. Relationships are built through opportunities for communication and teamwork. Best practices are applicable to all grade levels and provide the building blocks for instruction. Best practices motivate, engage, and prompt students to learn and achieve" (Public Schools for North Carolina, 2016).

We left Google and began talking to teachers, asking how they defined best practices. While most agreed a best practice is a practice with a research base that proves its effectiveness, we couldn't find two teachers who agreed on how many research studies it took to justify calling a practice a "best practice." When we'd ask what type of research (longitudinal, qualitative, quantitative) was required, the consensus answer was "I don't know."

When we asked why it's important to use best practices, probably the most honest answer came from the teacher who said, "Because my principal said we had to use them." When we followed up by asking her what practices the principal had decided were "best," she said, "We bought a textbook that said it was built around best practices and so we have to follow the textbook." When we asked teachers what best practices were appropriate for the entire school, most weren't sure, though some mentioned practices such as using positive reinforcement, handling discipline problems in a timely way, and encouraging meaningful homework. Others mentioned having professional development communities, using instructional coaches, or giving teachers time to plan together.

When we use the word *research*, we refer to both quantitative and qualitative studies by teachers and other researchers.

Best Practices: Followed and Ignored

In fact, when we have asked teachers to tell us which best practices they used, we found wide variance (see Chart F). In some places, teachers thought that having kids write paragraphs using the "hamburger method" was a best practice. (We disagree.) In other places, teachers said starting the school day with a "status of the class"

Chapter 10

meeting was a best practice. (We agree.) Some said that "giving kids time to read each day" or "writing every day" or "giving lots of feedback" or "using data to inform instruction" or "calling students by their names" are best practices. Each of those practices—if done right—is indeed something we'd easily call "best." But, again, when we pushed and asked, "Why is it a best practice?" the most teachers could give us was that some research supported it.

What we find confusing is that sometimes we all want to say we're doing research-based best practices, but other times too many of us are willing to ignore what we know from research. Almost one hundred years of research confirm that teaching grammar in isolation does not improve a student's ability to write a compelling paper and yet that practice is pervasive. Decades of research reveal that giving kids lists of words to learn to spell does not solve spelling problems, yet the Friday spelling test is an institutional rock that isn't budging. We know that purposeful writing, writing conferences, and writing portfolios are important, and yet too often teachers assign a topic, don't confer with students, and think a folder with all the writing collected into it is a portfolio.

Numerous research reports explain the critical importance of dialogic talk and yet most classrooms are still based in monologic talk (see Chapter 15 for a discussion on this topic). We know—we *know*—from research that giving kids choice in what they read is critical in increasing volume of reading (see Chapter 13) and that the volume of reading is predictive of reading achievement and yet school after school after school we visit still prescribes novels, doesn't offer choice, and is content if students read merely four required novels

SOME BEST PRACTICES IN READING

Give Choice
When we give kids choice in what they read, they are more motivated to read.

Increase Volume
Volume of reading that kids do on their own is an important predictor of school success.

Read Aloud
Students need to hear you read aloud a range of genres.

Teach Strategies
When students learn strategies to use while reading, they are more likely to become independent readers.

Model Thinking
Students will learn how you think through a text when you model your own thinking.

Encourage Classroom Talk
Classroom talk about texts improves understanding of those texts.

CHART F

a year. It seems that we turn to best practices some of the time and institutionalized—and unquestioned—practices at other times.

And too infrequently are we willing to venture into "next practices."

Next Practices

If a best practice is rooted in what has worked in the past, a next practice speculates about what might be better for the future. Luckily, some people in our history—both centuries ago and yesterday— were unwilling to rest upon best practices. These are the people who are willing to risk failure, as Eli Terry did when he conceived of interchangeable parts for clocks; as Henry Ford did when he envisioned a moving assembly line at which men stood still while the car being built moved past them; and as John Bardeen, Walter Brattain, and William Shockley did as they mastered the technology needed to create the transistor. All of them risked failure to create something new.

We think Nancie Atwell (1987) did that when she wondered what would happen if she turned her classroom into a workshop; Donald Murray (1980) and Donald Graves (1983) risked failure when they wondered what would happen if we looked at writing as a process; Marie Clay (1975) did so, too, when she changed our ways of observing children as readers and writers; Ken Goodman (1982) did so when he posited a more holistic view of learning to read and write based on the interdependent relationship of multiple cueing systems; Louise Rosenblatt (1938) did when she explained how meaning is made in a transaction between the reader and the text; P. David Pearson and Margaret Gallagher (1983) did when they (building on the work of Joseph Campione, 1981) suggested that students need more than explicit instruction and ongoing practice. They need instruction designed around a gradual release of responsibility from teacher to student.

What all these people have in common is that they set aside how things had been done and wondered instead what would happen *if*. They didn't wait for the world to change; they changed the world.

But most educators seem reluctant to head into next practices. We tend to wait until others have tried those practices often enough to create a history that proves them valid. Maybe that's because we've become an educational system guided more by fear of failure than respect for innovation. Kids worry about failing; teachers worry what happens if kids fail; principals admonish teachers to make sure kids don't fail; superintendents demand reasons for why a school is "failing." The public shuns the failing school.

If the goal is "don't fail," then the result, we fear, is "don't innovate."

> **If the goal is "don't fail," then the result, we fear, is "don't innovate."**

Fear of failure becomes a reason we avoid venturing into the unknown. New ideas rarely work the first time, so if we are to make changes, we have to accept the probability that our first efforts won't go quite as well as we want them to. The cleaning product Formula 409 is so named because the first 408 formulas did not work. There were 408 failures that preceded success. A *next practice*—that first attempt—hasn't yet been tried so it certainly isn't yet the best. And it may never become "the best." It may take a number of trials, some failed experiments, to finally find one or two that move from *next* to *best*.

Sustaining Next Practices

Some types of next practices are sustaining because we simply take what we're doing and make it better. We sustain, but we improve and innovate, too. That's what's happening in the current cell phone industry. If you're old enough to sing *Tie a Yellow Ribbon Round the Ole Oak Tree* from memory, then your first mobile telephone wasn't actually too mobile. It was big. In fact, that first cellular telephone was about the size of a shoe box, came in its own shoulder bag, and weighed 2½ pounds. Thank goodness someone moved to a next practice—a smaller, lighter phone—and a next, and a next. If your first cell phone was a flip phone then you skipped that early iteration of this ever-evolving device. But whenever you joined the cell phone world, and whatever model you own now, it's already on its way to becoming obsolete.

Other gadgets are evolving in a similar way. The icebox turned into the refrigerator, to which has been added the ice dispenser, *crushed* ice dispenser, food tracker, expiration-date tracker, grocery-list creator. The sustaining innovations make it better, but it's still a refrigerator.

Televisions might have become high-definition and flat, and their rabbit ears might have been replaced by the satellite dish, but they are still TVs. The push lawn mower became a self-propelled lawn mower. But it's still a lawn mower. The kitchen sponge evolved to be soap-filled and bristle-backed. But it's still a kitchen sponge. A sustaining next practice is all about building a *better* mousetrap. We embrace better mousetraps in education. There are few chalkboards left in classrooms, but digital projection systems still put images and words upon the wall.

Disruptive Next Practices

Building that better mousetrap couldn't happen, however, until someone had built the first one. That first one disrupted the practice of living, probably not happily, with a family of mice.

Disruptive practices are disruptive because they end one approach, probably a time-tested "best practice," and replace it with another. The creation of the transistor radio, light bulb, batteries, the home computer, and the Internet were all disruptive practices. Gutenberg's 1439 printing press, with its movable type, is, some say, the greatest disruption of all. All these disruptions shared a common trait: They changed the way we live. They changed our world.

But if not for a willingness to move from now to next, to wonder what's beyond yesterday's best, we'd be stuck. Henry Ford once said, "If I had asked people what they wanted, they would have said a faster horse." His quip shows the difficulty we have in envisioning change. We fear too many of us in education have difficulty envisioning change. We have lost that willingness to question what we have and conceive of something new, and to take the risks that "something new" requires. Too often, "I wonder what would happen if . . ." is countered with, "Prove it." "Could we try. . . ?" is answered with, "What's the research?" And "Wouldn't it be fun to . . . " is pushed aside with, "After the test." Our schools often seem to turn to a blend of best practices and traditional practices, too seldom trying radical and disruptive changes that might— or might not—actually transform teaching.

Innovation is the lifeblood of progress. It is nursed and nurtured in the arms of failure; in collaboration; in creativity; in curiosity; in passion;

in tenacity and grit and optimism. It does not let us merely survive; innovation is what lets us thrive. And innovators are what we need.

We're all figuring out what those disruptive next practices will be in schools. We brought in computers, but they all too often just made the workbook electronic. We added the Internet, but it all too often just gave students a faster way to search for information. We realized kids need to work collaboratively, but we still tell them what to work on and how long to spend doing it, too often on their own. In other words, we made a small disruption fit within a model of education we all know and understand. We talk of reforming schools, but that usually means writing new standards; it rarely means truly re-forming schools. Reforming schools begins with some serious conversations about topics we sometimes complain about, but rarely create the time to discuss seriously.

> **Innovation is the lifeblood of progress. It does not let us merely survive; innovation is what lets us thrive. And innovators are what we need.**

Turn and Talk

Take Two: Chapter 10
scholastic.com/
BeersandProbst

- What's an instructional or procedural practice you remember from when you were a student that teachers still use today? Is it worth keeping? Instructional practices relate to your teaching, whereas procedural practices relate to routines and rituals, such as the length of the class; the use of textbooks; pep rallies on Fridays, etc.

- How do you define best practices? What about your colleagues?

- What best practices do you follow in your subject area? Talk with colleagues from other subject areas. What are their best practices? Do you see any commonalities among your best practices?

- Are there practices you follow that cannot be supported by research? Why do you use them? Should you reconsider?

- What are some ideas you'd like to try? What's holding you back?

- What are some changes in educational practices that you would like to see, although they appear impossible?

Chapter 11

Reassessing Success

WE STOOD IN THE HALLWAY of the Hynes Convention Center in Boston after finishing our presentation at the International Literacy Association annual convention. As we stopped to make sure we had all our paraphernalia—computer cords, dongles, jump drives—a teacher asked if she could answer a question we had posed in the presentation, but she had been reluctant to answer before the whole group. We nodded. She said,

> "You asked, 'What guides most of the educational decisions at your school?'"

We nodded again.

> "Well, at our school, there is only one thing that counts: the state test, so there is only one question that is asked: Will this help students score better on the test?"

We all stood quietly for a moment. The teacher looked tired. And she looked sad. She went on.

> "I hate it. I hate that I agree to it. I hate that I don't stand up more. I hate it. But there it is."

Yes, there it was: That honest admission that, in too many places and for too many kids, we've let preparing students for tests substitute for promoting engagement. In too many places, we've let a test score become the measure of success of a school, of students, of individual teachers. When that happens, then test-prep packages promising higher scores become the curriculum for "pushables" (so named by a middle school principal who wanted teachers to focus on students who had scored a 2 on the mandated test, but with "pushing" could reach the acceptable 3 score) and "slipables" (yes, those students at risk of slipping from a 3 to an unacceptable 2). When that happens, we will have fallen into the trap Dov Seidman warns of in *How: Why HOW We Do Anything*

When that principal was asked about the kids who were scoring 1s, she said the focus should be on kids who could make or maintain the scores the school needed. We fear this means the 1s were "expendables."

Means Everything. In the preface he explains, "there is a difference between doing something *so as to* succeed and doing something *and* achieving success" (p. xxxvi), and many schools seem to confuse the two.

Losing Our Way

We see that confusion frequently. Someone decides that improved test scores are the best measure of success and so everything moves toward improving the scores. Teachers feel the pressure to make sure scores do indeed go up, so the focus of instruction turns to covering what's on the test. As one teacher told us, "If it's not going to help kids answer items on the test, I can't teach it." And so the test scores might go up, but what we truly value might not, such as interest, creativity, self-reliance, and passion for the disciplines.

Doing something *so as to* succeed may shift our focus away from what is central and most important. In education, it may shift focus from true learning to the measures of learning we have devised. Unfortunately, those measures may not be adequate. Doing something *so as to* succeed is also about responding to extrinsic motivation. That motivation might be to gain a reward (e.g., bonuses for the superintendent; "A" ratings for the school; job security for the teacher) or to avoid a punishment (e.g., public ridicule; student retention; teacher dismissal). In either case, extrinsic motivation requires a constant upping of the reward or punishment, which isn't sustainable over the long haul.

By contrast, doing something *and* achieving success generally means looking beyond that short-term goal (passing the test) to a longer-term purpose (becoming a lifelong, passionate, curious learner). Schools that focus on this loftier endgame are less interested in what it takes to attain a particular score and more interested in what creates engaged, motivated, self-directed learners. It's like dieting: If you watch what you eat just to be able to wear that special outfit for that special party, chances are that within a month of that party, that outfit won't fit again. But if you decide that you want to live a healthier life, want to make better food choices, want to exercise more, then not only will you get into the outfit, you also probably won't outgrow it again.

In *Drive*, Daniel Pink makes a statement similar to Siedman's. Pink says: "When the profit motive becomes unhinged from the purpose motive, bad things happen" (2009, p. 302). When the purpose motive for school is to help kids become confident, passionate, lifelong learners; to help them discover all they can be; to help them become ethical participants in society; and to instill some habits of mind that value compassion, curiosity, collaboration, and creativity, then the profit motive has less to do with high test scores and more to do with engaged students.

> **When the purpose motive for school is to help kids become confident, passionate, lifelong learners . . . then the profit motive has less to do with high test scores and more to do with engaged students.**

When schools focus less on test scores and more on engagement, we see positive effects: higher attendance rates, fewer discipline referrals; more student-generated questions; more comments that reveal inter- and intratextual connections; classroom conversations that are started and maintained by students; *and* higher test scores (Cotton, 1988). Focusing on the essentials in education, rather than on test scores, seems to result in higher test scores. Students become learners who take risks, who see questions as things to be explored and not merely to be answered. They graduate with a sense of self, with an understanding that they have valuable contributions to make, with content expertise, and with both the open mind that lets them take things in and the critical eye that allows reflection, analysis, and evaluation.

But if the profit becomes nothing more than a higher test score, the focus of instruction shifts. Questions have to be answered, correctly. Risk-taking is only for the gifted, and then, only when their scores will not be jeopardized. Curiosity, collaboration, and creativity are for the unit *after* the test (but even then those units often are only for the gifted). Lifelong learning, as an associate superintendent told us, "isn't really my goal. I just need kids to pass the test. It's all about the test." When the profit motive becomes unhinged from the purpose motive—Pink is absolutely right—bad things do happen.

Those *Other* Kids

In far too many schools, we've been willing to accept as our critical measure of success the ability to improve a damned test score. To make this matter even more disturbing, it appears to us that test-prep instruction is almost exclusively the instruction for our underachieving students. And in this country, those students are most often our students of color (Fordham & Ogbu, 1986; Harper, 2010; Thompson, Warren, & Carter, 2004).

Our students who come from homes of affluence, or if not affluence, at least homes with enough—enough money *for* a home; enough money for breakfast and lunch and dinner; enough money to buy the novel the teacher wants kids to read; enough money to get to the store to buy the poster board or the calculator or the soccer cleats needed the next day—those students have parents who would almost never agree to scripted lessons, formulaic writing, skill-and-drill curriculum; and test-prep lessons.

Such experiences are for *those other* kids. The belief that some kids should receive less to help them achieve more is a bias that must be examined. Such action, or lack thereof, results in a segregation of intellectual rigor that must be called out for what it is: a racism hidden behind the genteel admonition that "those kids need this kind of support"; that "those kids just can't handle this type of freedom in the classroom"; that "those kids can't discuss why a character acted in a particular way until they can name the character."

Such diminished educational experiences are less often experienced by children who come from homes where parents know to demand more. More creativity; more critical thinking; more relevance; more collaboration; more technology; more choice; more conversations; more focus on comprehension strategies that create independence.

Do we mean to suggest that children of poverty do not have parents who question a test-prep-driven educational experience for their children? No. We have watched countless parents show up for conferences sometimes begging, sometimes demanding to have their child placed in a classroom with "a better teacher" or "more meaningful work" or "where she will do something more than sit at a computer taking tests" or "where he'll get to make something" or "be with someone who will see what a great artist he is." We've heard plaintive requests for children to be allowed to have an education that is, at its core, about teaching that is not controlled and measured by test scores.

And when those requests are made, they are, far too often, met with "We've got to get those scores up" or "That class is for students who have

Bob: Kylene wrote "The Genteel Unteaching of America's Poor" when President of the National Council of Teachers of English. Go to scholastic.com/BeersandProbst to read this Presidential Commentary.

shown they can do the work" or "This is what our assessments show your child needs." Occasionally we've seen one child put into another classroom, and we've watched that child thrive. But the others—the other parents who couldn't miss work one more day, who couldn't find the bus fare to get to the school, or who trusted the refrain "this is what is best for your child"—found that their child stayed in a classroom in which things were done *so as to* succeed on a test. And too often, those kids left in those test-prep classrooms become apathetic, uninterested, disengaged. They might (or might not) pass the test, but even if they do, that one measure of success is a poor measure of educational benefit and a poor predictor of lifetime learning.

> **Differentiation must be grounded in equity, in access, in agency. Differentiation that results in a diminished educational experience for *those* kids is not only wrong, it is shameful.**

Yes, too often, under the guise of "differentiation," students are given less. Differentiation must be grounded in equity, in access, in agency. Differentiation that results in a diminished educational experience for *those* kids is not only wrong, it is shameful. It is a form of segregation that must be examined, exposed, and rejected. All students deserve an education that engages and motivates, that inspires lifelong curiosity.

Hijacked by Tests

If we want to shake the educational universe, we need to think disruptively. We need to ask ourselves those two questions we have mentioned a couple of times now:

- What needs to change?
- What assumptions make that change hard?

Thinking about how we measure success at a school may require that we challenge a deeply entrenched system of testing and a huge and powerful testing industry. If your school has been hijacked by tests, then you'll have to be willing to say to yourself, your students, and their parents that we will help all kids become empowered learners, and we will no longer be guided by a test-prep mentality. Taking such a stand will almost certainly be uncomfortable, but it's essential.

We aren't asking you to refuse to give any more state-mandated tests. You don't have the authority to take that stand, and we aren't asking you to defy your contractual obligations. That said, you might find it interesting to read about districts that have cut back on tests (Kamenetz, 2015) or have asked their State School Board to eliminate high-stakes tests (*Katy News*, 2015). We are asking you, though, to think about how some curricular decisions in your building and in your classroom are made. You can help change your school culture regarding testing even when you can't change the school test. Explore with your colleagues your school's attitudes toward testing by discussing the questions that follow.

Poet Sara Holbrook takes on Pearson testing as she discusses the questions about her poems Pearson has included in some high-stakes tests, questions she, the poet, can't answer. Read her comments at scholastic.com/BeersandProbst.

Turn and Talk

- If we visited your school and went on a tour with you and others, what would the visible signs and artifacts say about what is most valued?

- How is student growth monitored in your school? Is there a data-room in your school? This is a place where every child's scores from all the tests are visible for all to see. If so, what's the purpose of this room? Who visits this room? Can students see it?

- What type of pressure do you feel to improve **test scores**? What pressure does the administration in your school or system feel? Have you ever worried about doing something in your classroom because your principal might question if it is a best practice, or might question if it will improve test scores?

- How many meetings do you attend weekly or monthly to discuss in some way how to improve or monitor student test scores? Are students discussed as "pushables" or "slipables" or some other such terms? Do students with lower test scores lose electives or recess to attend classes designed primarily to improve those scores?

- What makes you feel powerless at your school? What would help you feel empowered?

- In three years, what would you like your school to be known for? What needs to happen this year, next year, and that third year for that to happen?

Take Two: Chapter 11
scholastic.com/
BeersandProbst

Chapter 12

Rethinking Relevance

"BUT IT IS SO DAMNED HARD to get kids interested."

We couldn't argue with the teacher who said this. We actually have thought the same thing many times. Creating interest, building engagement, is so very hard. There is so much competition, after all: videos, video games, text messages, Instagram, Snapchat, WhatsApp, Tumblr, Twitter, sports, and occasionally even the real outdoors. When kids can go to YouTube and watch, well, just about anything, learning about bees (not the birds and, just the bees) can seem tame at best, irrelevant at worst.

But if we could make it relevant, then teaching would be easier and, we hope, learning would be more interesting. To get there, we need to begin by challenging a confusion we've noticed. We think far too often we have confused the words *interest* and *relevance*. In *Reading Nonfiction*, we wrote:

> *Interest* is about something out there, out in the world. The video is interesting. The photographs are interesting. Interest is often fleeting, lasting about as long as the video clip we provided for kids to watch. *Relevance*, by contrast, is always personal. Relevance is about what matters to you. It starts with observing something in the world, but then it shifts to a thought or a feeling inside of *you*. Something that is relevant is inherently interesting; but something that is interesting isn't always relevant. In short, getting kids' attention is about creating interest; keeping their attention is all about relevance (2016, p. 45).

We believe this confusion of terms is the root of many frustrations teachers sometimes feel. We all work hard to begin a new unit with something that ought to create interest. And it does. But that interest quickly wanes and we feel that once again we must put on a show to recapture our students.

Students' interests shift as quickly as a Snapchat message appears and disappears, so if we're going to base engagement on interest, we're going to have to work very hard. But if helping students recognize the relevance of a topic means ultimately they will be more engaged and invest more energy in the lesson, then eventually we will spend less time on building interest and more on helping kids discover the relevance of the material we offer them. And when they discover the relevance, their energy for and attention to the task will soar. Getting their attention is about interest; keeping their attention is about relevance.

Kylene: Bob has often said, "Rigor resides in the energy and attention we bring to a text." I'd add that it's about the energy and attention we bring to a *task*." **Bob:** I'll accept that revision. Kylene says that rigor without relevance is simply hard. We've made a mistake in beginning a conversation about raising the rigor without a having a conversation about developing relevance.

> When they discover the relevance, their energy for and attention to the task will soar. Getting their attention is about interest; keeping their attention is about relevance.

Getting to Relevance

We were sharing these thoughts in a workshop when a fifth-grade teacher spoke up as we paused. She said she agreed with us and then added, "But I can't always worry about relevance because I've got a curriculum I've got to cover. Some things just won't be relevant. And, even if I had time to worry about relevance, I teach sixty-eight students throughout the day. How am I supposed to help each see relevance in what I've got to teach?"

When she finished, we asked how many others felt the same frustrations. Many hands went up, and one stayed up.

A young teacher—who we later discovered was doing her student teaching and was here for her very first workshop—offered a hesitant comment: "I don't want to contradict anyone, but when I was in middle school, we were all always asking why we had to learn this or that. The answer was always, 'It's what the curriculum says we have to cover.' And when I was in high school, it was even worse. No one cared what we wanted to learn. If it wasn't something that would help us on the state test, we didn't do it. School was just so very boring. I decided to become a teacher because I wanted to be the teacher who helped kids discover what they want to learn. But all of you are making me think that I'll end up doing to someone else what teachers did to me as I make kids study something in a book or for a test or in a curriculum guide. I don't want to be that teacher."

"I don't want to be that teacher." Her words stung. We all knew that from time to time we had been that teacher.

The first teacher spoke again: "I hate the teacher I've become so I'm really asking: How do I make what I've got to cover relevant to all these kids who have such different experiences?"

Kylene: You probably can't.

Bob: Well, you probably can't if some things stay the same.

We hated saying that to those teachers. We hate writing it here. But in our experience, it's the hard truth. We told the teachers that as long as a preset curriculum guides our decisions, we will have a difficult time creating the learning environment that develops passionate learners. We're interested in schools that would be thought of as intellectual communities, those places where students burst through the doors each day, eager to question, to discover, to try, and even to try again when they fail. We want students to graduate dismayed at the thought of leaving behind this part of their life that has been set aside to explore, to create, to learn. That is more easily and more genuinely achieved if the question begins, "What do kids want to know?" rather than "What does the curriculum say we must cover?

What Do Kids Want to Know?

The naysayer in that workshop rolled her eyes and said, "Great, we'll be discussing critical questions like, 'Should we have homework?' and 'Why can't we have longer recess?'" We will set aside the fact that we think those are actually fine questions for kids to ask and turn to what we think she might have been wondering: What types of issues might kids want to explore?

That's a great question and we decided to find out by creating an online poll asking students in grades K–12 that very question. Additionally, we asked how long they get to work on those problems while at school. We were stunned at the issues students brought up. Look first at a representative sampling of what high school kids mentioned:

- "Solving all of the hate in the world. So many people commit suicide and hurt themselves because of people bullying them."

- "Terrorism, and ISIS in particular, are a major threat to the world. We can let terrorism make us live our life in fear or we can solve it."

- "Racism in America. Everyone should be treated equally no matter where you came from or what color your skin is."

- "The problem I would like to solve is discrimination towards people with mental illness. Lots of people have some sort of mental illness and I wish that we would learn how to be accepting of people with them and to not bully them."

- "Protection of wildlife and their environments because each year more and more species become extinct or added to the endangered species list due to the destruction of their habitats."

- "A problem I would want to fix is to stop raping and trafficking of woman and children."

- "I think the biggest problem in the world is fixing the environmental problems because if we don't fix global warming and pollution, thousands of species could go extinct and the whole food web could be messed up."

We ran an online survey for students grades K–12 for one week beginning October 4, 2016. We had 1,090 students respond. We discuss this survey more at scholastic.com/ BeersandProbst.

Many of these same issues were echoed by middle schoolers:

- "I would like to work on poverty, because many people that are poor don't deserve it and should have a chance to be able to drink clean water."

- "I would like to work on solving the refugee crisis around the world—helping refugees get supplies and homes."

- "I would like to raise adoption awareness because my sister was adopted. When she was in the orphanage, she was not treated very well. I want the number of kids in orphanages to go down in my lifetime."

- "Racism. It's important because most of the past has been based off of it, causing many unnecessary problems. Today racism still negatively impacts us."

- "I would like to eradicate slavery around the world. This is important to me because it is heartbreaking to think of families and kids not being able to experience the joy of being free."

- "I would really like to solve world hunger. This is important to me because here in America people eat lots of food and some people in Africa don't get a chance to eat some days."

- "I would like to solve the problem of cancer. This is because it is constantly killing people."

- "Stopping the violence. It's important to me because there is way TOO MUCH violence."

- "Depression. I want to make sure no one suffers from sadness. It's important to me because I know what it feels like, and it's not a good feeling."

When we looked at the responses from upper-elementary students, we found their thinking was just as global, though we began more often to hear phrases like "because I'm afraid" or "because I'm worried":

- "Violence because if there weren't violence, you could go up to people you don't know and feel safe being where you are and asking for help. Right now I don't feel safe."

We cheered the loudest for the middle school girl who wrote, "One problem I would like to solve in the world is the things that kids are taught in school. They don't help us solve real problems."

- "Bullying. Everyone should feel amazing about themselves. No one deserves to be bullied or treated differently or mean."

- "I want to solve the water problem because it makes me scared worrying that some people have to walk a long way with a bucket just to get water and what if that happened here."

- "Clean up trash. We are destroying our future by making the environment a not so safe place."

- "The world for me is peace and kindness because hurting or doing something bad to somebody is wrong so if everyone was nice and kind that would be AMAZING!"

- "I want to make sure there are more women scientists in the world because girls should be able to be scientists, too, not just boys."

- "Saying hurtful things and bad words. This is important to me because when you do bad thing or say bad things, it makes you look bad and I want to change people from doing that."

- "Poor people because it's sad that they don't have a lot of money or food to eat."

- "Bad guys because I worry."

- "To donate food to people who don't have food. Because people get hungry and could die from having no food."

- "Getting people not to judge other people by their skin color. Even though people might have different cultures, they're still people."

Though the kindergarten through second-grade students had slightly more concrete tasks in mind, like their older counterparts, they are interested in making something better:

- "Fix having buildings always catching on fire. Because I don't want people to die."

- "Picking up garbage because there is garbage all around and it is bad for the earth."

- "Find out why dogs get worms. So dogs won't have them anymore."

And we laughed the most at the reply of the boy who misread the prompt (we think) and said, "My biggest word problems to solve are the ones in math. They are the hardest."

While some students misspelled words, their passions were easily understood: "Plases are geting palotid." "To mutch litering." "Suisid." "Bules must stop."

- "Global warming. Because it's not going to snow any more, and the ice is melting, and there isn't ice for the penguins and polar bears and they are all going to die and I don't like that."

- "Pollution. Because then the world would be more beautiful and we would be healthy."

- "Fish. I like to eat fish, but there aren't many fish to catch. They are gone! Just GONE."

- "I want brown skin and peach skin to get along and I want everyone to be nice to animals."

These examples make us want to stand and cheer. While we all worry that students are spending too much time interacting with a screen, it just might be they are looking beyond the most recent text message or tweet to the larger world. We hate seeing young people afraid of terrorism and ISIS and worried about global warming, world hunger, and racism, but we love that they believe they can have a hand in solving these problems. They haven't left the difficult issues for someone else. They aren't responding, "I can't do anything" or "I didn't make the mess so it's not my problem" or "I wouldn't know how to begin." They want to *solve* these problems.

Next, we asked these students how much time they get to spend at school working on big world problems. Of the students we surveyed, 49 percent responded, "Never," while 27 percent said, "Not too often." Only 24 percent said that they work on these problems "Some of the time" (17 percent) or "All of the time" (7 percent). We wonder how much easier it would be to create relevance if we started by working on the problems kids actually want to solve and the issues that concern them. And if we did focus on some of those problems, there would certainly be a great many opportunities for both reading and writing, and so we could continue to teach the skills we have always considered to be important.

In too many places, the curriculum for the second decade of the 21st century still looks far too much like the curriculum of the mid-20th century. Sure, we've added technology, but kids are still inundated with learning that was better suited for a world that wasn't as rapidly changing as this one. We know it's hard to let go of educational practices that require kids to memorize states and capitals, practice cursive writing, label the steps in the water cycle, identify types of rocks, or label the different regions of North America—all examples of tasks expected of third graders in school districts across the country in 2016. "Letting go" might well be a critical skill for educators in this fluid and rapidly changing world.

Relevance in the Curriculum

What intrigued us most in this list of issues, problems, and concerns generated by students was the weight and significance of all of them. Students mentioned poverty, racism, climate change, human trafficking, pollution, and other similarly serious problems. These are the same issues adults worry about. Very few trivial items—wearing costumes the entire month of October or more video games for all—made their list.

> "Letting go" might well be a critical skill for educators in this fluid and rapidly changing world.

The longer we looked at their concerns, the more we saw the potential link between the classroom and the curriculum. Virtually every one of the items suggested to us texts students might be invited to read and the sort of writing and talking they might be encouraged to undertake.

Several students mentioned racism, for instance. A long list of writers and books cascaded through our minds as we read that. *Stella by Starlight, One Crazy Summer, Warriors Don't Cry, Henry's Freedom Box, A Handful of Stars, Baseball Saved Us, My Name Is Bilal, Separate Is Never Equal, Brown Girl Dreaming, The Watsons Go to Birmingham–1963*—all these books might hold interest to students who want to think deeply about racism.

Many listed global warming as a problem they want to solve. That phrase alone reminded us of countless articles we have seen in newspapers and magazines, and—more usefully for elementary school teachers—in publications like *Scholastic Scope* magazines, and on websites such as newsela.com. Kids can read nonfiction including *The Down-to-Earth Guide to Global Warming; World Without Fish; Seymour Simon's Global Warming; How We Know What We Know About Our*

All the books, magazines, and articles for children we reference in are listed on page 171.

Students remind us that when learning is relevant, engagement is high and students are excited to learn.

Changing Climate; Basher Science: Climate Change; and *DK Eyewitness Climate Change.* A year's worth of reading and writing could emerge from those two words alone.

All that is simply to say that the issue of relevance is relevant. It can shape the way we choose texts for students, the way we invite students to choose the texts that they will read independently, and the approach we take to all of that reading. The issue of relevance reminds us that the work children do in the classroom should be significant to them, not simply preparation for something significant they will undertake years in the future. If they are to undertake anything significant in the future, it will be because they have learned the importance of significant work early on in their schooling.

We are chastened by the suspicion that we had been working backward. We took our curriculum and its goals as a given, and we tried to make our students appreciate what we had to offer. We had a curriculum, and our job was, so we thought, to get students interested in it. Even when we moved beyond that, and tried to make it relevant for them, not just transiently interesting, we may have been overlooking the obvious. We suppose that it is possible to convince someone of the relevance of some issue. But it is probably far easier, and more natural, to identify what is already relevant and begin there. That seems especially true when what students see as relevant is of undeniable significance.

Okay. Again, we're climbing down from our soapbox. We were, frankly, excited to climb there. To rethink relevance, to seriously reconsider who is in charge of determining relevance—us or them—means shaking the foundation of a lot of teachers. As one high school AP literature teacher told us, "You simply cannot expect that I would ever, ever give up teaching *Heart of Darkness*. That is unthinkable." Well, yes we would.

But we also know that disrupting our thinking about interest and relevance might require having potentially difficult conversations with our colleagues. Perhaps these questions will help.

Turn and Talk

Take Two: Chapter 12
Take a look at one student's award-winning video to see relevance in action: scholastic.com/ BeersandProbst

- What assumptions about relevance need to be discussed in your school?

- Why do some teachers hang on so tightly to what's been done in the past?

- Have you asked your students what issues matter to them? If not, why not? If so, what did they tell you?

- Do you have some assumptions or biases about letting all students work on solving big real-world problems? If your main concern is that pressure from passing "the test" gets in the way, ask yourself what you would be doing differently each day if there were no high-stakes test to shape your instruction.

- Where do you want to be three years from now regarding relevance? What small steps this year could lead you to where you want to be in three years?

Chapter 13

Silent Reading

WE ARE STUNNED to be heading into the third decade of the 21st century still finding ourselves needing to make a case for sustained silent reading in classrooms. And yet we do apparently need to make that case. Consider this conversation with an elementary school principal:

Bob: How much time do kids spend reading silently each day?

Principal: I really don't know. I'm sure that some teachers give kids some time each day to read.

Kylene: Don't all teachers require that kids read on their own each day?

Principal: No. We don't see the evidence that silent reading helps. In fact, there was a big report that said that. I'm surprised you don't know it.

We told the principal we did know the report she had in mind and suggested she look at it once again because what she thought the report said wasn't what it actually said. She assured us she'd give it another look and then went back to asking us what we could do to help improve test scores in her building. We said that the work would begin with all kids reading, each day, every day, at school. She said she was looking for someone who could really help with test scores. We nodded and said that improving how well students scored on reading comprehension began with kids reading. She nodded and tried again, "But the real focus needs to be test scores." We decided we were probably not the best fit for her school.

If you want kids to be better readers, they must read. And if you want them to read a lot, much, perhaps most, of what they read must be what they choose to read.

Oral Versus Silent Reading

Our very earliest classrooms in the United States focused more on oral reading than silent reading for a couple of reasons. Sometimes there simply weren't enough individual hornbooks and, later, books to place one in each student's hands. More often, though, the teacher wanted to make sure that pronunciation and expression were correct. The teaching of reading was the teaching of decoding, and the teacher needed to hear the child decode words in order to assess the reading.

If you want kids to be better readers, they must read. And if you want them to read a lot, much, perhaps most, of what they read must be what they choose to read.

Then, as *thinking* about the teaching of reading began to emerge, the question of oral versus silent reading moved center stage, or at least it did for people who sat around the newly invented light bulb to discuss such issues. Early-reading researcher Edmund Burke Huey questioned how readers understood what they were reading. His book *Psychology and Pedagogy of Reading* (1908) argued that silent reading was "the art of thought getting" (in Pearson & Goodin, 2010, p. 13). He believed that it was during silent reading, not oral reading, that students had the opportunity to think about what was being read and to decide, on their own, what the text meant. Other researchers began to look at how silent reading meant faster reading and allowed for students to think more about content as they read. As such, in the reading research circles, silent reading gained a voice.

But that didn't mean it was catching on in schools. Children were still reading orally since teachers still felt they needed to hear if they were pronouncing words correctly.

The focus on pronunciation continued with the introduction of a particular early-reading basal. The escapades of Dick, Jane, and then baby Sally, along with Father and Mother (who never had an escapade), were shared through the Dick and Jane basal K–2 reading series, popular from the 1930s through the 1970s. This series taught generations of children how to read by focusing on the look-say or sight word approach. Students practiced the words they had just learned as they read silently

Kylene: So, Bob, did you read all of Huey's book?

Bob: Absolutely. Didn't you?

Kylene: Didn't you also read a welding manual?

Bob: I did! Loved it, too.

Kylene: Right.

and then the practice would move to oral reading so that the teacher could assess pronunciation and prosody, though we aren't sure what expression best suits "See Dick. See Jane. See Dick and Jane." Disbelief? Cajoling? Utter boredom?

Interestingly, even though this series required silent reading of the stories, what occupied the most time in classrooms was their oral reading. Round Robin Reading (RRR) became the norm throughout the 20th century as children sat in circles or in rows and read aloud, one child at a time (Beach, 1993). Someone finally figured out that children were simply counting how many students sat before them, counting down to the paragraph they would have to read when it was their turn so that they could ignore

> **Round Robin Reading became the norm throughout the 20th century as children sat in circles or in rows and read aloud, one child at a time.**

everything that came before and after the moment they were on the spot. When they realized that, teachers tried a new approach: Popcorn Reading. Now, teachers would just skip around the class, calling on anyone at any time. What should have kept all the students on their toes, following along, just raised the anxiety level of the class, especially for those students who hated to read aloud.

Today, despite common recognition that RRR (or its cousin, Popcorn Reading) invites boredom and anxiety and doesn't build comprehension, the practice continues (Kuhn, 2016). Some teachers have always embraced it, saying RRR allows them to assess how well students can call the words (Opitz & Rasinski, 1998). Others continue the practice because it allows them to hear how fluently and expressively a child reads a passage (Rasinski & Hoffman, 2003). Others—more often in science and social studies classes—have said that RRR is the easiest way to make sure that students read everything in the textbook (Armbruster & Wilkinson, 1991). Finally, other teachers turn to it because it was how they learned to read.

But for whatever idiosyncratic reason any one teacher gave, the reality was the same across the country: Round Robin Reading was the prevalent mode of reading in the classroom.

Silent Reading Emerges

During the late 1970s, some teachers (finally) began to question this practice and turned to silent reading. Two events encouraged this shift. First, in 1967, the Elementary and Secondary Education Act (more recently known as NCLB) provided federal dollars for the purchase of books for school libraries. This dramatically increased the number of books that many children had access to during the school day. Second, beginning in the last part of the 20th century, more and more children's books, as well as books in a newer field called young adult literature, were being published. The number of books available for students increased dramatically. So, not only did schools have a new source for books, but there was a growing body of books in the school library from which to choose. And with the increase in what students could read came a new practice in the classroom: sustained silent reading (SSR).

> Today, despite common recognition that RRR invites boredom and anxiety and doesn't build comprehension, the practice continues.

Weekly trips to the school library began to take place and time to read during the day (or at least week) became commonplace. Whether called SSR or DEAR (Drop Everything And Read), beginning in the early 1970s and extending through the early 2000s, teachers were, more than ever before, giving students time to read in class. Reader's workshop, as described by Nancie Atwell in her landmark text *In the Middle* (1987, 1998, 2014), provided a context for making silent reading a significant part of pedagogical practice and not simply a Friday afternoon respite.

The National Reading Panel's Report

Then, in 2000, the nation—well, at least reading teachers in the nation—was surprised when the National Reading Panel issued its report that said (among other things) that there was not enough evidence to be found in the research studies they had reviewed to state conclusively whether SSR improved, or hurt, reading comprehension. What was heard by many educators, though, was not that message, but

The principal we mentioned on page 124 was referring to this report.

rather the message that SSR does *not* improve reading. The NRP report was interpreted to show that silent reading has no value. And that created a gasp that was heard around the world, or at least throughout reading journals, literacy conferences, and school hallways.

That finding, based on fourteen studies that the NRP found to meet its criteria for review, did *not* conclude that silent reading was *not* valuable. Nor did it conclude that it *was* valuable. The report simply said the panelists couldn't draw any conclusions about silent reading based on examining those fourteen studies. But many restated that absence of any finding as a finding that they expressed in a shorter quip: "reading does not improve reading." That interpretation was allowed to stand when Timothy Shanahan, then president of the International Reading Association (now called the International Literacy Association), wrote in his president's message that "research doesn't show that encouraging reading improves reading, and that sustained silent reading (SSR) is probably not such a good idea" (*Reading Today*, 2006, p. 12).

Policy makers and principals used the NRP report to build a case against time spent reading silently in classrooms, arguing that valuable instructional time should be spent on instruction and that if kids were to read more, they should do so at home. Today, many years after the report's publication, the two of us visit schools that do not participate in SSR because "the policy says we can't" or "research says it doesn't work" or "it's just not allowed." When we ask, "What research?" or "Who wrote the policy?" or "Who doesn't allow it?," more often than not, we're met with blank stares. One teacher told us, "Last year was my first year in this school. I had kids reading silently, and my principal stopped by and told me to stop wasting instructional time. When I said I thought it was important, he said that 'a report said it wasn't.' And so based on 'a report' we can't do it.'"

What the Report Said

We suspect the principal was referring to the NRP report. We wished he had done more than accept the quip "reading doesn't improve reading" and instead questioned what the report actually said.

Other researchers and reviewers have looked at the fourteen studies the NRP examined and the thousands it bypassed. Those folks have offered strong evidence that the studies examined were flawed or that,

> Personal email with Timothy Shanahan reveals that he supports SSR when it is accompanied by meaningful instruction. We agree.

had other studies been examined, evidence would have conclusively shown the importance of SSR (Fisher, 2004; Garan & DeVoogd, 2008; Reutzel, Fawson, & Smith, 2008; Trudel, 2007). Rather than review all those studies again, we want to look more directly at the definition of silent reading that the NRP used. The NRP looked at studies that

1. gave students time to read each day.

2. let students choose what they read.

3. did not provide any sort of supervision.

The report explains that, in studying how comprehension improves, the panel wanted to look at the practice of letting students read silently:

> "Another, less explicit, but widely used approach, is to encourage students to read extensively on their own or with minimal guidance and feedback. Programs in this category include all efforts to increase the amounts of independent or recreational reading including sustained silent reading (SSR), Drop Everything And Read (DEAR), Accelerated Reader (AR), and various incentive programs. Often these approaches have no formal name, but take the form of requirements that students engage in unsupervised independent reading" (NRP, 2000, p. 3-1–3-2a).

While all of us might recognize the joy of doing something with no supervision, with no guidance, with no feedback, we suspect most of us would agree that supervision, guidance, and feedback are what offer us a better chance for growth.

So the NRP looked at studies in which students did "unsupervised" reading with "minimal guidance or feedback" and then was surprised when there was no evidence that this affected reading ability. If that's not worth a gasp of disbelief, then it's at least worth a "you've got to be kidding."

While all of us might recognize the joy of doing something with no supervision, with no guidance, with no feedback, we suspect most of us would agree that supervision, guidance, and feedback are what offer us a better chance for growth. If we want to get better at something, then some help, some sort of direction, is probably needed. Do we want kids picking up a book from time to time at school just for fun; with no supervision; with no reason to read other than that they want to know something or want to get lost in the mystery or get caught up in the adventure? Of course.

But the silent reading instructions that Nancie Atwell encourages in *In the Middle* (1987, 1998, 2014) or *The Reading Zone* (2007, 2016), that Linda Rief discusses in *Read Write Think* (2014), that Penny Kittle discusses in *Book Love* (2013), that Kelly Gallagher discusses in *Readicide* (2009), as well as the thinking we encourage in *Notice and Note* (2013) or *Reading Nonfiction* (2016), are approaches that are far from unsupervised and unguided. They provide plenty of feedback to students. Those silent reading programs might better be called reader's workshop or what we call focused silent reading (FSR).

Focused Silent Reading

Focused silent reading, as seen by the observer standing in the classroom doorway, would look a lot like, as one principal said to us, "kids simply reading." When we asked that principal if that was problematic, he responded, "Yes. They are just reading. I think I need them doing something." We pointed out that they *were* doing something—they were reading. "Yes," he said. "But how do we know what they are thinking?"

The principal is right. With focused silent reading, the kids are all reading. They might all be reading different books, or two or three might have chosen to read the same book. And we won't know what they are thinking unless we ask them. But they will have *chosen* to read that book. And the fact that they have chosen the

Books arranged alphabetically rather than by a reading level give children the widest range of choice.

book probably indicates, at the very least, that they are willing to think about it as they read. Their choice will not have been guided by a reading level, but by interest. And—when needed—it will have been selected with the teacher's assistance. Choice means choice. And asking a student what he wants to read doesn't begin by asking that student "What's your reading level?" A better question might be, "What do you want to think about?"

The lesson, if the observer arrived early enough, probably began with whole class instruction. The teacher explained what she wanted students to focus on this day as they read. For developing readers, that might be a fix-up strategy to use when they encounter a new word. For any reader, it might be a lesson on how to notice if a character is changing. It might be a lesson on how to read with expression, or when to back up and reread or sketch a picture if a particular passage is confusing. It might be a lesson on the importance of noting text structure or word choice or the author's use of evidence in building an argument. You teach. You model. You let them practice with you watching. And then you send them off to read what they choose to read. And as they read, you circulate, checking to see if they are applying what you've just taught.

Simple prompts can help teachers quickly assess if the time spent reading that text in class is well spent:

- Tell me what's happening now in your book.
- Tell me about the person telling the story.
- What's the most surprising thing that has happened?
- Are you enjoying the book? Why or why not? If not, is this a good book for you to continue reading?
- What have you learned so far about the character (or event)?

Then, to figure out if the focus lesson is being applied, the teacher asks the student to show her an example of the application of that lesson. If she's taught the signpost Contrasts and Contradictions, she might ask the student to point out an instance of that text feature and talk briefly about what it showed them. Or if she's taught them to be aware of transition words, she might ask them to explain how those

The number one question we're asked is, "Where can I find books for kids?" We share ideas at scholastic.com/BeersandProbst.

words connect different parts of the story. Or she might simply ask them how they figured out how to understand an unknown word.

And after reading, if our observer has stayed long enough, he might see kids writing notes about what they've read in their reader/writer journal. Or, maybe he'll watch kids turn and talk with a buddy about the skill they practiced as they read. Or perhaps he'll see the teacher pull the whole class back together to ask students to share how they applied today's focus lesson. Focused silent reading recognizes that the time we have with kids is valuable and so we should spend it wisely. And that begins with reading. Reading for sustained periods of time. Reading what you choose to read. And reading with focus.

Reading at School: Why It Matters

Often, we're asked if kids could just read silently at home so that school can be a place for "things other than reading." The problem with that idea is that not all kids have access to books in their home, not all kids have parents who support reading at home, and not all kids have the time or will make the time to read at home (see Chart G).

The disparity between who has access to books and who does not falls along poverty and ethnicity lines. The 2016 report *Library/Media Centers in U.S. Public Schools: Growth, Staffing, and Resources* by Tuck and Holmes found that wealthy schools with primarily white students have five times more librarians/media specialists than high-poverty schools with mostly students of color (p. 5).

> Wealthy schools with primarily white students have five times more librarians/media specialists than high-poverty schools with mostly students of color.

The national average for visiting the school library is once per week. So, on average, if you have 100 students in one week, there would be 100 visits to the library. This holds true *except* in high-poverty schools where that number drops to only 80 visits per 100 students (p. 11). In the wealthiest schools, 61 percent of school librarians allowed students to access libraries before or after school. That number dropped to 48 percent in high-poverty schools (p. 11).

Some Resource Needs Grow as Poverty Levels Increase

Across each of these three areas, educators in high-poverty schools are more likely to say several critical resources and circumstances needed for student success are NOT adequately available for their students.

Educators Who Say Each Item Is NOT Adequately Available for Their Students, by School Poverty Level

Outside-of-School Resources & Environment:
Access to fiction/nonfiction books at home

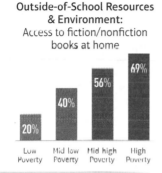

Family & Community Engagement:
Family involvement in student learning

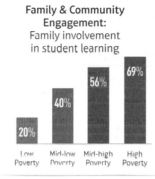

In-School Resources & Environment:
Programming that includes the arts, foreign languages, etc.

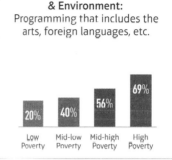

CHART G

Additionally, educators report that in highest-poverty schools, 69 percent of their students don't have access to fiction or nonfiction at home (Scholastic, 2015).

And yet, we know that children with parents who are barely literate do as well in school as children whose parents have university degrees *if* the homes have 500 or more books for children (Evans, Kelley, Sikora, & Treiman, 2010). Put another way, children who grow up in homes with no books tend to be about three years academically behind children who grow up with books (and that's after controlling for issues such as income, home language, and parents' educational level) (Jumpstart, 2009). Additionally, children who live in impoverished neighborhoods are essentially living in "book deserts," places that lack community libraries, quality books stores, and other places where parents can find books for their children (Neuman & Moland, 2016).

These disparities are more than unsettling when viewed alongside the research that reveals the benefits of high volumes of reading (see Chart H). The reasons to increase the volume of reading from birth through high school are numerous and compelling. When decision makers are convinced of the importance of reading, they often ask how much time should be spent reading each day.

9 REASONS TO READ MORE

Builds Knowledge
Cunningham & Stanovich, 2003 • Pressley, 2000

Improves Achievement
Allen, Snow, & McNamara, 2015 • Anderson, Fielding, & Wilson, 1988 • Allington, 2012 • Blachowicz & Ogle, 2008 • National Assessment of Educational Progress Report, 2015 • Worthy & Roser, 2010

Increases Motivation
Atwell, 1987 • Feitelson & Goldstein, 1986 • Guthrie, Klauda, & Ho, 2013 • Ivey & Broaddus, 2001 • Lapp & Fisher, 2009 • Lesesne, 2003 • National Endowment for the Arts, 2007

Increases Vocabulary
Krashen, 1989 • Nagy, Anderson, & Herman, 1987 • Nation & Cody, 2013 • Read & Hodges, 1982

Improves Writing
Bazerman, 1980 • Goodman & Goodman, 1983 • Langer & Flihan, 2000 • Raphael, Kirschner, & Englert, 1988

Builds Background Knowledge
Anderson, 1984 • Anderson, 1985 • McVee, Dunsmore, & Gavelek, 2005 • Ozuru, Dempsey, & McNamara, 2009 • Smagorinsky, 2001

Improves Understanding of Text Structures
Armbruster, 2004 • Fletcher, 2006 • Kendeou & van den Broek, 2007 • Meyer & Rice, 1984 • Snyder, 2010

Develops Empathy
Allington & McGill-Franzen, 2013 • Bal & Veltkamp, 2013 • Johnson, 2012 • Koopm & Hakemulder, 2015 • McLean, Breen, & Fournier, 2010

Develops Personal Identity
Abodeeb-Gentile & Zawilinsky, 2013 • Begum, 2014 • Fives, Russell, et al., 2014 • Hall, 2012 • Harste, 2009 • Jesweak, 2015 • Tatum, 2009

CHART H

How Much Is Enough?

To answer how much reading is enough, consider the Anderson, Wilson, and Fielding (1988) study. It showed that fifth graders who were in the 98th percentile read 65 minutes a day outside of school. This meant that in a year, they saw around 4.3 million words (see Chart I on next page). By contrast, students in the 70th percentile were reading about 10 minutes a day and thereby seeing only about 622,000 words in a year. Students at the 50th percentile were only reading about five minutes a day and were therefore seeing only about 282,000 words in a year. And students at the 30th percentile were reading at a bare minimum of 1.8 minutes a day and were seeing only about 106,000 words.

Then Adams (2006) took that study and figured out what would happen if each student added only 10 minutes a day of reading (see Chart I). The student who would have seen about 106,000 words in a year reading just under two minutes a day would be exposed to 556% more words over the course of a year by adding 10 minutes of reading a day. And students reading at a little more than 21 minutes per day would see nearly 1 million more words in a year by adding 10 more minutes to their daily reading.

Connecting children to books begins with showing them the books that mean a lot to you.

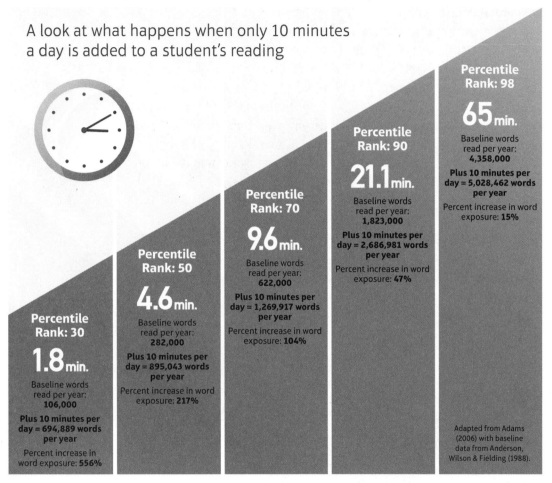

A look at what happens when only 10 minutes a day is added to a student's reading

Percentile Rank: 30

1.8min.

Baseline words read per year: **106,000**

Plus 10 minutes per day = 694,889 words per year

Percent increase in word exposure: **556%**

Percentile Rank: 50

4.6min.

Baseline words read per year: **282,000**

Plus 10 minutes per day = 895,043 words per year

Percent increase in word exposure: **217%**

Percentile Rank: 70

9.6min.

Baseline words read per year: **622,000**

Plus 10 minutes per day = 1,269,917 words per year

Percent increase in word exposure: **104%**

Percentile Rank: 90

21.1min.

Baseline words read per year: **1,823,000**

Plus 10 minutes per day = 2,686,981 words per year

Percent increase in word exposure: **47%**

Percentile Rank: 98

65min.

Baseline words read per year: **4,358,000**

Plus 10 minutes per day = 5,028,462 words per year

Percent increase in word exposure: **15%**

Adapted from Adams (2006) with baseline data from Anderson, Wilson & Fielding (1988).

CHART I

Ten minutes. Ten minutes a day of focused silent reading has the potential to change a child's academic life, and that might, in turn, change her life's trajectory.

Giving kids time to read is necessary, not optional. And giving them the chance to discover what they want to read is also necessary. When schools choose not to do those things, they are simply failing to provide a good literacy education. And that is a bad choice.

Turn and Talk

A friend of ours liked to say that great teachers have the patience of a saint and the persistence of a sinner. We have always chuckled at that, while recognizing the truth of her statement. We think it might be even more appropriate when thinking about starting a focused silent reading program. To get you started, consider these questions.

Take Two: Chapter 13
scholastic.com/
BeersandProbst

- Are you satisfied with the amount of silent reading that happens in your classroom? In your school? If not, what's keeping you from requiring more reading? If your answer is "policy," remember, you can't have a conversation with a policy. Can you engage the author of the policy in a conversation? What points would you raise in that conversation?

- How much reading do you do on your own? What helps you get started in a new book? What helps you keep reading when other distractions appear? What do the reflections on your own reading tell you about what we ought to do for our students?

- Reading logs often get in the way of reading, but students do need a place to record what they are reading, how many pages they cover each day, and perhaps their thoughts about it. We also think keeping a list of what to read next is helpful. What reading logs have you seen that you like? What hasn't worked in some logs that you want to avoid?

- What do you say to administrators or parents who might suggest that when kids are "just reading," you aren't "really teaching"?

- Where do you want to be in three years with a focused silent reading program? What steps do you need to put into place now to get there?

Chapter 14

Reading the Same Book

A FIFTH-GRADE TEACHER said to us, "But don't we all need to read the same book at the same time? I did in school, and I turned out just fine."

We answered her question with a question:

"Do you believe it's important to give your kids choice in what they read?"

She answered almost immediately. "Of course it is. They can read what they want during choice reading time. But they do need to choose books from my library and they do need to choose books within their Lexile level. But other than that, of course I think they should get to choose. But I also think that we need to all read the same books throughout the year."

Choice Means Choice

Choice reading does not mean choosing a book within a certain Lexile level or color range level. Choice means choice. Does that mean we don't ever give kids time to read something we know is at their instructional level? Of course not. We have kids read at their instructional level when we are instructing, when we have taught a skill that we want them to practice immediately. If we're in a school that uses guided reading, then during the guided reading time with a small group, of course those students will be reading a text at their instructional level. But we don't think it serves any children best if they never have the chance to choose what they want to read. At the same time, it's important to note that the choice won't be unsupervised. Also, we want to avoid situations in which children believe that they, not a book, are a level. As a taxi driver in New York City said to us in response to hearing what we do, "Can you help me? Our grandson is an H. We don't know what an H is. But his teacher keeps saying he is an H and should be higher." No. A child is not an H. But giving children choice doesn't mean abdicating responsibility in helping kids choose.

From Kylene: I walked around the room doing a quick check of reading logs, the place where students recorded each day how many pages were read that day. I noticed that Tam, a fourth grader, had made little progress in the book she was reading:

Kylene:	You have read about fifteen pages in your book in the past two days. What's going on?
Tam:	I don't know. It's really hard.
Kylene:	What's making it hard?
Tam:	It has really hard words.
Kylene:	Could you read a part of this paragraph to me?

Tam began reading slowly, laboriously, with no inflection, stumbling over most of the words. I stopped her after a sentence or two.

Kylene:	Why did you choose this book?
Tam:	My sister said it is good. I thought my parents would be impressed if I read it, too.
Kylene:	What grade is your sister in?
Tam:	Eighth grade.
Kylene:	Can you tell me what happened in the part you just read to me?
Tam:	Not really.
Kylene:	Do you like this book?
Tam:	Not really.

I convinced Tam that she might enjoy another book more. She happily agreed. But if Tam had claimed she loved it, didn't want to stop reading it, and understood what she was reading, then I probably would have told her to keep reading. Or if she did not understand it but desperately wanted to keep reading it, I might have looked to see if she could listen to it as an audio book while following along. After listening to it, we'd check to see if her understanding had improved. If so, her desire to read it might make it worth allowing her to continue listening while following along in the text. I'd want her to get through it as quickly as possible so I could get her onto another book she could read with less difficulty. I know that kids need to read a lot, read with understanding, and read what they choose. I can guide and I can remind kids to let go of book that isn't working for them, and when they want to read the popular book—or in Tam's case the one she thought would please her parents—then I want to help figure out how to make that reading experience work as well as it can.

In fact, kids report that their favorite books and the ones they are most likely to finish are the ones they pick out themselves.

We know this contradicts others who would say kids must always read only within their instructional level. We disagree. Instructional level reading most certainly has a place and a function during the school day; but choice reading, done during focused silent reading, is valuable and should not be dismissed (see Chart J). In fact, kids report that their favorite books and the ones they are most likely to finish are the ones they pick out themselves (Scholastic, 2015).

The Same Book

We think the teacher who asked if kids should ever read the same book deserves an answer. To answer her question, we want to begin by saying that no one is asking us if we should ever have a class-wide reading of a shorter text—a poem, an article, a short story. All of us would probably say yes to that question. Instead, we are most often asked if it's appropriate to spend weeks and weeks with everyone in the class reading one novel. This question, to be clear, is rarely

What Kids Want in Books

Children across age groups overwhelmingly agree that their favorite books—and the ones they are most likely to finish—are the ones they pick out themselves.

Children's Agreement With Statements
Base: Children Ages 6–17

"My favorite books are the ones that I have picked out myself"

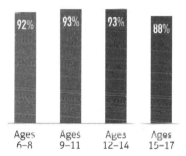

"I am more likely to finish reading a book that I have picked out myself"

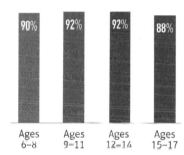

Total Kids **91%**

Total Kids **90%**

CHART J

important to ask in primary grades, where teachers read aloud a cornucopia of books to children—some short, some long. They read aloud what they know children will love and they read aloud to help children develop what Eudora Welty once called "a reader's ear." This question about everyone reading the same book, at the same pace, to answer the same questions, begins to emerge around fourth grade.

Occasionally, the question is hopeful: "I remember how much I enjoyed the weeks when our entire class read *A Tale of Two Cities* in eighth grade. Don't you think it's important to make sure kids read some books as a class?" Sometimes, the question is skeptical: "Surely you aren't one of those people who thinks everyone in class should read the same book at the same time?" But, honestly, most often we are asked this question by teachers and parents who are confused and just want some direction.

Some direction is about all we're able to offer. Here's what we know:

First, in early primary grades, teachers read aloud short texts—picture story books and short chapter books—to create for many students a deep love of reading. And in those same grades, that expected time each day when the teacher reads a chapter from a beloved book provides an entrance into the world of longer literary experiences. But those shared reading moments of early years are balanced by children reading on their own, or with a buddy. They serve a far different purpose from the teacher in later years who wants all to march through *The Scarlet Letter* at the same pace.

Second, in later school years, everyone reading the same book at the same time won't actually provide a positive reading experience for all. For many, it will be so negative that not only will we have failed to improve comprehension and fluency, but we will have created a dislike of reading. Any woman will tell you the label "One size fits all" is a lie. Nor will one book fit all.

And third, too often class-wide reading of a novel takes too long. Our 2014 survey of 478 teachers grades four through eight revealed that, on average, teachers spend six to eight weeks reading a novel with students. Neither of us can think of one novel we want to read for eight weeks. If we love the book, we want to devour it. If we hate it, we want to quit reading or at least want the torture to end quickly.

These two boys chose to read the same book.

Chapter 14

When the intensive study of a single novel over several weeks is compared with reading that novel more quickly, and then moving on to read other independently chosen novels—in other words, extensive reading—the intensive study does not result in higher comprehension of that novel. But intensive study of a novel does result in more negative attitudes toward reading (Coryell, 1927; McConn, 2016). In other words, intensive study of a single novel does little good and perhaps significant harm.

All too often, class-wide reading of a novel becomes a read-aloud event for the class, for any of several reasons. The teacher may feel a need to keep everyone moving through the novel at the same pace, or think that some students can't read the novel on their own. Listening to an audio book has great benefit, especially in building vocabulary, improving comprehension skills, and fostering a positive attitude toward reading. Listening to a book while following along has some benefit in improving decoding.

> **Listening is not reading. There is value in listening, but listening uses and hones different skills from reading.**

We believe that this shared oral experience of a novel is different from the experience students have when silently reading the same novel at the same time. Listening is not reading. There is value in listening, but listening uses and hones different skills from reading.

So Why Ever Say Yes?

When we consider those facts, we can't support the class-wide reading of a single novel enthusiastically. We're trying to create passionate, lifelong, inveterate readers. Class-wide reading of a single novel won't accomplish that for too many readers. But we also know that many times we have enjoyed reading the same book someone else is reading. We love talking about it. We want to compare favorite passages or talk about parts that surprised us or ask each other questions about why a character did this or that. We like the community that is created as we share our reading. We like learning from one another. And we see the same impulse in our students. Too much right now seems to be about dividing us. Don't we need some common experiences that unite us? Isn't the sharing of literature one of the most powerful ways to unite?

It's our hope that the solitary act of reading might become a social event, one through which we learn together, that compels us to say, "Yes, from time to time, we ought to come together to read the same novel." To make this as positive an event as it can be, we offer these guidelines.

Guidelines for Class-wide Reading of the Same Book

Read the same book, but don't expect all students to read it the same way.

We think the problem isn't that we all read the same book; it's that we expect all kids to read it the same way. We all must be on chapter two at the same time, answer the same questions, have the same conversations. Expecting this uniformity is the problem.

Kylene: In the spring of 2016, the two of us agreed to read *Most Likely to Succeed* (Wagner & Dintersmith, 2015). Bob immediately downloaded it to his Kindle. I bought the print version. He read it in the evenings, with a glass of red wine. I read in the evenings, too, with a glass of white wine. I read it in one or two sittings. Bob digested it in smaller chunks. I wanted to talk about as I was reading. He preferred (he mentioned several times) to wait until he was done. He mulled over specific sentences, sometimes focusing on individual words as he wondered why the authors chose this word and not that one. I read first for the bigger picture and then returned to do that more leisurely mulling. (It's amazing we get anything accomplished together.) My point: We're a class (okay, it's a small class) that has chosen to read the same book, but we read it in different ways.

Use the time that students are reading for one-on-one conferences.

We know many suggest that when students are reading you should model your own love of reading by opening your book and reading along with them. While there are days when you want to say (and probably ought to), "I know I'm supposed to have a conference with some of you now, but I just must keep reading for another ten minutes," we encourage you to use this time to have one-on-one or very small group conferences with students. Use this time as instructional time to see if students need help with something they've read, are applying a lesson you've taught, are using fix-up strategies when confused, can point out a favorite or confusing passage, have ideas about what will happen next, and so on.

There's lots to be discovered as you talk with students for three or four minutes. For many days in the school year, that silent sustained reading time for your students might be the only time you have for reading, too. But this time is better spent in conferences with students. And remember, if you can make the time to read at home, you can enjoy that reading with your favorite cup of tea or glass of wine, red or white, as you prefer.

Give students a voice in choosing the in-common book.

The two of us often read the same book at the same time. Almost always, that book we choose to read is agreed-upon. Neither of us would be happy with an assignment from the other. We decide we want to read a professional book, so we look at what's new and make a choice together. Or we go to Amazon and find the next great post-apocalypse novel, a genre sure to make us feel better when we're behind on a deadline. We are reading the same book, but we've chosen to read it. As often as possible, narrow your selection—perhaps you will narrow it to two, or perhaps three—and let students choose as a class the novel they all will read. It won't make everyone happy, but it will probably make than them happier than if you simply assign the title without paying any respect to their opinions.

Don't confuse listening with reading.

If you choose such a difficult a book for students that they are struggling through it, then recognize that you aren't improving decoding or building fluency or helping any other aspect of their reading. If your solution is to read the book aloud to students, then you might improve listening ability, and you'll certainly model fluent, expressive reading, but this solution does not offer students the needed practice of reading on their own. Listening doesn't build reading stamina; listening doesn't allow the reader to decide when to reread, when to untangle a confusion, when to mull over a favorite passage, when to stare at illustrations. Listening doesn't allow the student to take responsibility for the reading. But it does allow us all to experience the text together.

> When we think about how kids read, we know that how they read is tied to how much they read and how much they read is connected to wanting to read.

If students will be listening, it's best if they have a copy of the text in front of them and are following along. Plus, it's best if you are the one reading it to them. Practice the pages you'll be reading aloud each day. If students will be listening to a recorded version, it's best if you're sitting there, holding your own copy, listening with them. And, finally, don't choose a book that will take four weeks to read aloud. You want to finish the book in a week.

When we think about how kids read, we know that how they read is tied to how much they read, and how much they read is connected to wanting to read. That desire is best nurtured in schools that haven't confused test prep with education, that have rethought what relevance means, that provide big blocks of time for kids to read, and that recognize that giving kids choice in what they read isn't restricted to a particular level.

Turn and Talk

- How do you handle different ways of reading the same book?

- How do you make the reading of an in-common book comfortable for students at different ability levels? How do you avoid slowing down the faster readers, and avoid embarrassing those who read more slowly?

- In your school, do you give students choice over in-common reading? Would that be possible to do?

- When you have kids reading an in-common book, what else do you have going on in the classroom? Does work on that book occupy all of your time, or do you integrate it into other instruction?

- Do you find ways of connecting the in-common reading to the individual choices students make for further reading? How might you do that?

- Where do you want to be in three years regarding class-wide reading of the same book?

Take Two: Chapter 14
scholastic.com/
BeersandProbst

Chapter 15

The Power of Talk

WE THOUGHT IT IMPORTANT that a chapter about the power of talk start with us sharing some talk between the two of us. It's a written conversation, shared via email, but it's at least a conversation.

Kylene: What was talk like in your classroom when you started teaching?

Bob: When I started teaching my biggest problem with talk was stifling it. My students weren't reluctant to talk. They came into the room talking, kept on talking over one another and me, and left the room still talking when the bell rang. In the hallways, during that five-minute break between classes, it seemed as if everyone in the entire school was talking at one time. And loud.

I worked hard to make talk what I thought it ought to be, and ultimately I got the kids whipped more or less into shape. There were exceptions, of course, and constant backsliding, but in the classes in which I felt reasonably successful, the talk began to look more and more like the image I held in my novice and naïve teacher's mind:

- The classroom was quiet and I was in control.
- I did most of the talking, which was as it should be, since I was the teacher and supposedly knew more about whatever topic we were addressing than anybody else. I knew that I, at least, had actually done my homework and read the assignment.
- The kids talked only when I called on them.
- I called on them primarily so that they could answer a question I had devised. (Occasionally, when I hadn't had enough time to prepare a decent lesson plan, I might ask, "What did you think about what you read?" but I always felt that such an open, ambiguous question was an admission of laziness on my part.

I hoped the department chairman wouldn't drop in when I knew I was going to fall back on such an unscripted question.)

- I called on students if they raised their hands properly, with no exaggerated waving or accompanying sound effects, and I had some reason to expect an answer that wasn't ridiculous.

- When they answered, they talked to me, not to one another. That, again, was as it should be. After all, I had asked the question, so I was the one to whom the answer should be directed.

- I was the one to evaluate the answer, which I usually did with a wise nod or a disapproving grimace, which the class understood to be "right" and "wrong," respectively.

- Students didn't bother to listen to each other's answers, unless that answer was being offered by one of the two or three brightest kids in the class, and then they might want to write the answer down in case the question showed up later on an exam, or if they knew that the student answering was probably going to get it so wrong that I would call on someone else to answer the same question, and thus they might want to be prepared just in case I happened to choose them next.

> **Kylene:** These few pages are our exact email exchanges. This bullet point might reveal why Bob isn't great on Twitter.

- Actually, no one had to listen to much of anything because they knew that several minutes before the bell rang I was going to say something like, "Thus we have seen. . . ." What followed that introductory phrase was going to be the point of all the preceding forty-five minutes of interrogation, a point that I knew we would get to because I had devised the entire lesson to go precisely there and nowhere else.

Kylene: You were working from the assumption shared by a lot of teachers, including me, and a great many administrators—that teacher-directed talk is the most productive and efficient. As a beginning teacher, you probably had a lot of good reasons for holding that assumption:

- You were probably taught to write inductive lesson plans, which meant that you sketched out a series of questions that would help kids move from confusion to comprehension. After doing all that work, of course you naturally wanted them to answer your questions.

- Your department chairman, principal, and supervisor probably expected you to run the class, to be in charge, to control the pace and the content, to demonstrate good classroom-management skills.

- Your teacher's manual probably gave you an impressive list of questions to ask students, and you knew that if you didn't direct the conversation, you'd never get around to all of them.

- Probably the only alternative to directing the class that you could imagine was chaos.

Bob: Maybe. I think it's just what I thought I needed to do. What about you?

Kylene: I think that early on, I thought talk was about students answering my questions. Actually, I probably thought "talk" was for the hallway. "Discussions" were for my classroom, though very little was actually ever discussed. I am positive that early on I didn't see talk as a part of the comprehension process and the discussion was for sharing what you had already comprehended.

Bob: I made that shift, too, from talk that is to share what's understood to talk that is to help students create understanding. I wish I had made the shift sooner.

Obviously, we both struggled with talk in our beginning years of teaching. The pretense at conversation was simply the method for communicating the content. Ideally, the students led through that pseudo-inductive talk would also learn something about reasoning, but that was probably wishful thinking. We, the teachers, were the ones who had set up the path the thinking would take, and all the students had to do was fill in the blanks left for them. Beyond the filling in of the steps, they didn't have to do much reasoning themselves.

And then, of course, our students had to make a note of that final summary statement. That's really all they had to listen to. All of the talk was designed to get to that point. If they woke up in time to write that down, they would have the essence of the lesson, the conclusion to which all those carefully designed and inductively arranged questions led.

Classroom Conversation and Real Talk

So conversation in the classroom was not much like conversation anywhere else. It didn't meander, it didn't explore, it didn't have any of the mutuality and reciprocity of real talk, the kind we engage in after we've seen a good movie or a bad political tweet. A simple comparison with any conversations we've ever had with friends makes that obvious. Those conversations were different in almost every respect:

- No one was in control—instead, we shared the responsibility for raising questions and suggesting possible answers.

- No one person did most of the talking. Instead we went back and forth.

- Nobody was calling on anyone—we spoke when we had an opening or when we absolutely couldn't restrain ourselves from interrupting.

- When we had questions, they were real questions—we weren't checking the other's comprehension of the text.

- Those questions seldom had simple answers, easily labeled right or wrong. We didn't answer them, so much as explore them. The question, "What did you think about it?" didn't seem lazy in this context. Rather it often seemed the appropriate question, the one that would invite people in and open up the talk.

- If the conversation involved more than two people, we all listened to everyone. We wanted to hear what the others had to say.

- No one got to say, at the end, "Thus we have seen. . . ." Although we may have argued for a position, we were content to let all participants arrive at their own conclusions.

Talk in the classroom had little in common with talk outside the classroom. The talk after we had read the homework assignment had little in common with the talk we had after we had watched a movie together. We doubt that much of the talk that went on in our classrooms, during those first days or years of teaching, did much to prepare students for the talk that they would undertake once they had left our schools.

PART III

For the classroom talk to serve as good preparation for the talk that students will engage in later, we may need to disrupt our conceptions of talk in several ways.

Monologic and Dialogic Questions

The easiest way to look at our classroom talk might be to consider the nature of the questions we raise. We might distinguish between monologic and dialogic questions.

By monologic, we mean the sorts of questions to which there is a right, or best, answer. They can be useful in checking to see whether or not the students were actually paying attention. Do they know the name of the main character? Can they identify the antagonist? What color was the hero's hat? All those questions can be answered correctly or incorrectly, and the teacher presumably can assess them quickly. You can quickly decide if the question you are about to ask is monologic by simply asking yourself if you already know the answer. If you do, it's a monologic question and you are asking simply to see if students know what you already know.

Dialogic questions, on the other hand, are questions that may not have quick and easy answers, but are usually much more discussable. You don't know the answer before you ask the question. "What's the best course of action for the hero to take?" There may not be one right answer for that question. Instead, the students might discuss the potential good and bad outcomes of alternate possibilities. To convince them that there is one right answer and many wrong answers for such a question would be to do students a disservice. Far better to teach them that there are ambiguities and uncertainties in the world. Whatever course of action the character takes, he will choose it not because it is the only course of action—the right course of action—but because it seems better than the others. In other words, there is no one correct answer. Dialogic questions offer us the chance to teach kids to look for evidence and provide reasons, but they seldom give us the opportunity to label answers right or wrong. When we ask students, "What surprised you?," they must have read the text, but we can't respond to their answer with, "Well, no, that didn't really surprise you. Who can help Timmy out here with a better surprise?" Dialogic questions are seen by kids as real questions and because they are real, students are more engaged and listen more to one another as they answer. Furthermore, they tend to answer in complete sentences as they provide explanation for their thinking (Cotton, 1988).

Shifting the Focus

Although the dialogic questions may, at first, be ones that we raise for our kids, they should also serve as invitations to the students to raise their own questions. They shift the focus slightly. Rather than ask the students to attend exclusively to the text, dialogic questions encourage them to consider the effect the text has had upon them. It focuses on the interaction of text and reader, and in doing so it welcomes the reader into the process. The reader is not asked to ignore himself in a sterile exercise of extracting data from the text. Instead, he is encouraged to look at himself, and at his own responses, without losing sight of the text. Thus, our first and most reliable question for students is simply, "What surprised you?" That requires him to pay attention to his own reactions as he remains alert to what may come as a surprise, but it also demands that he pay attention to the text so that he knows what it was that caused the reaction.

Similarly, the question, "What did the author think I already knew?" asks the student to be alert to that moment when she feels the need of more information, which again requires her to look at both herself and the text. She has to pay attention to the text so that she sees where she lacks necessary knowledge, but she has to articulate the gap in her own understanding. Text and reader, both, are essential in dealing with that question.

And our third major question, "What changed, challenged, or confirmed your thinking?," asks the student to look at the significance of the text for himself. It invites—maybe even encourages—reflection on his own understanding, his own values, his own conception of himself and his place in the world.

We hope that our students will develop the habits of looking closely at the text, considering carefully the impact it has upon them, and reflecting on the obligations all of that thought incurs. We hope that they will see reading as an opportunity to change, not just as idle amusement or a chance to collect facts and data. The last questions we think should be asked after reading a book, although it is often too demanding and difficult to deal with, are, "How has this book given me an opportunity to change and improve who I am? How has this book disrupted, if only slightly, my conception of myself and my thinking about the world?"

We need not abandon all that we have done in moving, if we wish to do so, toward this vision of reading as the opportunity to grow, to change, to become something more than we were. But we might want to shift our emphasis, placing it more firmly on the meeting ground between reader and text.

A Dialogic Conversation With One Teacher

We have shared our thinking about the importance of dialogic questions in other books, so it isn't surprising that during workshops we are often asked about this topic. One fourth-grade teacher's comments have been echoed by others across grades:

Teacher: I like the idea of asking dialogic questions, but don't I need to start with making sure they have the details down first? If I don't do that with some of my students, they might not ever remember the names of the main character.

Kylene: Maybe. [I looked at this teacher and she seemed close to my age. I thought she might have read some of the same books I had read.] Did you ever read *Bridges of Madison County*?

Teacher: Oh my gosh. I haven't thought of that book in years. I certainly did read it. I loved that book.

Kylene: Me too. What did you think of the ending?

Teacher: Oh my gosh. I was crying. And I was really conflicted. I wanted her to go with him. And I wanted her to stay. I remember thinking then that there have been times in my life that I've had to make choices that weren't actually what I wanted to do but I knew I should do. I felt like that's what she did. I hated the ending but that's what happens sometimes. It's not always happily ever after.

Kylene: I know what you mean. And what was the main character's name?

Teacher: What? Um. Hmm. I don't know. I don't remember. What was her name?

Kylene: And yet you remember the book. You remember being conflicted. You saw how that book had meaning in your life. You understood what some might say was an important theme of the book. Now, how much of this conversation we just had about the book would have happened if I had led with, "What was the name of the main character?"

Teacher: Oh. Oh my gosh. But I do that to my kids all the time. Is that what you mean? I never saw it this way. Never.

Kylene: I think we all do. We all want kids to know names of characters, but I'm not sure that's an important lead-off question. It's important for writing the essay; it's important for writing the book review; it's even important if there are too many characters being discussed and we need to keep them all straight. But monologic questions rarely open up exploration of thoughts, of feelings, of ideas, of connections. If we want kids to read closely, we have to let them get close to the text. And that usually begins with a dialogic question, in this case, "What did you think of the ending?"

Reread this conversation thinking about the BHH framework.

Assumptions About Talk

We fear that the greatest assumption we make in schools about talk is not to make an assumption at all. Do we ever consider how talk helps students become engaged, deepen understanding, explore nuances, learn to listen, learn to change, learn to rethink? Chaotic talk isn't the answer. Teacher-directed talk isn't either. The practice of having students turn to one other student and briefly talk with a buddy is a good idea and certainly a precursor to longer, student-led conversations. But none of that will happen until we each think about how we encourage meaningful talk in our classrooms.

Actually, we worry that for too many students reading will continue to be something that they dislike, something that is to be finished rather than enjoyed, something that is a school-time activity and not a lifetime endeavor. If we don't stop to have the conversations about the biggest issues we've explored in this text, we know that making the changes we need to make in many schools will be next to impossible. But we must make those changes if we believe that reading ought to disrupt our thinking. Our democracy requires that we be thoughtful citizens and if for that reason alone, we must find ways to make sure reading is an important part of a child's life. Getting there begins with the conversations you have with colleagues in your school. So once again, we ask you to turn and talk.

Take Two: Chapter 15
scholastic.com/
BeersandProbst

Turn and Talk

- What can you say about the questions you ask students?
  To answer this, you might tape one of your classes. Then consider the questions you raised:

  - ◆ Were your questions monologic (that is to say, you knew the answer before you raised the question), or dialogic (a question to which you did not know the answer, and which implied respect for the unique position of the individual reader)?

  - ◆ Did your students answer the questions, or explore them? In other words, are the questions quickly answered and dismissed, in order to move on to other matters, or did they lead to tentative answers, speculation, possibly even changing one's mind about an issue?

- Do you find yourself asking your lower-performing students more monologic questions than dialogic questions?

- Do your students enjoy the conversations that take place in your classroom? How often do you give them time to offer feedback about what they liked and what they wish could change?

- Do you have a list of questions for children to answer before a discussion begins? An outline? Or do students set the topic and raise the questions?

- As students participate in conversations, do they look mostly at you or at others? Do they raise questions or do they wait for you to raise them?

- What are the characteristics of great conversations you have with friends? Are those characteristics visible in your classroom conversations?

  - How much of class conversations do you direct and control?

  - How much of the conversation followed the interests and the questions of the students?

- Where do you want your classroom to be in three years with regard to talk? What would you like it to look like, sound like? What do you need to do this year to get started in that direction?

AND WHERE THE STORY GOES NEXT

THIS BOOK WAS WRITTEN with you and your students in mind. We don't have our own classrooms anymore, but we think it is critical that if we write about teaching then we must actually teach. So, when principals or teachers invite us into classrooms, we go. We teach kids. We try something new. We sit shoulder to shoulder with you when the lesson turns out poorly—because that sometimes happens— to figure out what to do better next time. We try to answer your questions about how something worked when the lesson goes well. We learn beside you, and that learning always informs our work. Without you, without your willingness to open your doors to us, we could not do what we do.

While our work in multiple classrooms does not give us what the majority of you have—a year of getting to know one group of children well—it does give us the chance to know what's happening in schools throughout this nation. Because of work that carries us to rural schools and urban schools, to primary schools and high schools, to the poorest schools and some of the wealthiest schools, to public schools and charter schools and private schools, to the smallest districts with only two or three schools and to the largest districts that bus more kids daily than are found in some states, we have a view of what's happening across the nation that we know others might lack. That perspective demands we reject sweeping claims from any politician or policy maker who declares our nation's schools are failing. Such generalized indictments are not only wrong, they are shameful. Once those men and women have walked our nation's schools' hallways, taught in those classrooms, worked with teachers, listened to principals, and sat beside students as they teach them something new and difficult, then they can make proclamations; until then, we'd prefer they not.

Do we see problems? Of course we do. We know you do, too. Do we meet some teachers who should leave this profession? Yes. Maybe you've met some of them, too. Are there schools that are struggling? Yes. But is the whole system failing? No. As our friend and colleague Hal Foster said, "America's schools work; they just don't work for all kids." And that's the problem. They don't work for all kids. A great education shouldn't be a result of living in the right neighborhood. It shouldn't happen because a student is assigned to one particular teacher. And it certainly shouldn't be left to the luck of the right lottery ticket that lets this student but not that one into the better school on the other side of town. A child's education is too important to leave to chance.

> **A child's education is too important to leave to chance.**

We want to ensure that when people read about the successes of a school, those successes are not tied to a zip code. *All* children in *every* school deserve an education that inspires curiosity, encourages creativity, requires critical thinking, urges collaboration, and nurtures compassion. All children deserve robust school and classroom libraries. All children deserve a curriculum filled with fine arts. All deserve science labs, engineering labs, coding labs, and language labs. All deserve history classes that explore the past so that we understand the present and can perhaps avoid pitfalls in the future, and they deserve math classes that develop their ability to reason as well as compute. All deserve language arts classes filled with purposeful writing, choice reading, and compelling talk. All deserve physical education classes that let children run, play, and develop strong bodies. All deserve buildings that all too often only our wealthiest enjoy. We have never understood a city that will allow some schools to sit in abject disrepair while others, perhaps only a mile or two away, look like the campuses of small elite colleges.

We write this conclusion thinking of Manuel. We met him several years ago, in a school in San Antonio, Texas. The school was in an impoverished neighborhood, and the principal and teachers had worked hard to turn it into nothing short of an oasis. The younger children all but ran into school each day, and even the older ones with their "I'm cool" look, arrived grinning widely. We taught our lesson and thought it went well. After the lesson, all the kids left, except one boy who stayed behind to help us straighten desks.

We had noticed that he had been quiet during class, doing little we had asked. So we thought it interesting that he was now obviously lingering to talk. We asked him how he thought we did teaching the lesson. "Okay, I guess." We asked him how we could change it, to make it more helpful for other kids. He replied, "I don't know." We waited. He finally said, "You seem like nice people and all, but I'm not sure how what you said is going to help me get off this street." He said that as he raised the Venetian blinds that covered the view of a brightly decorated asphalt lot: the school's playground. Beyond that was an empty field that had not been mowed in a while. The buildings across the street were old and some had graffiti on their walls. The area looked tired. We suddenly felt tired, too.

Manuel stood there, not angry, not rude, just resigned. The look in his eyes was a look no kid should have. He went on:

> "My parents come here to make sure me and my brothers get a good chance at a better life. They work hard. My dad has two jobs and my mom has a job that is six days a week. I want to do something to help them. I want to help them. But every year is only about make sure you pass the test. I want to do something to help them. I want to get us off this street."

The dream of one little boy: to help his parents. The dream of two parents: to help their kids. And the place those dreams can come true: in our nation's schools. But for that to happen, we must begin to think about big issues: the practices we embrace, what relevance really means, how we share books with children, what talk should be in a classroom. We need to recognize that reading ought to change us. Reading ought to lead to thinking that is disrupting, that shakes us up, that makes us

> ## Disrupting thinking sets us on a path to change, if not the world, then at least ourselves.

wonder, that challenges us. Such thinking sets us on a path to change, if not the world, then at least ourselves.

Reading as a Changemaker

To change, we have come to believe, is the fundamental reason for reading. And this is what we need to teach our students. If a changemaker—as a person—is one who inspires, who offers creative solutions to social problems, who mentors, who collaborates—then we see no reason why texts should not be viewed as changemakers. They *can* be viewed as changemakers if we recognize that we read for a far more critical reason than to be able to answer someone else's questions; we read to raise our own questions. We read to explore, to wonder, to grow, to become what we did not even know we might want to be. We read to change.

Change is, at least, the fundamental reason for the serious reading we do. In the realm of nonfiction, it is the reading of (or listening to) political speeches, research articles, commentaries on economic issues, editorials about public policy, and the like. For our youngest students, it is reading to learn about the world and the people in it. All of those texts we read to sharpen our thinking and improve our understanding or, in other words, to change ourselves. The reading we do in those early chapter books and later literary novels and poetry we encounter, from Maurice Sendak to Beverly Cleary to Laurie Halse Anderson and Robert Frost, we do to deepen our insight into ourselves and perhaps into human nature in general. That reading changes us. Or rather, it enables us to change ourselves, because we wouldn't want to hand over the responsibility for what we become to someone else, whether a persuasive novelist, an eloquent preacher, or a convincing politician. Presumably, we want to be able to define ourselves, rather than have our lives sketched out for us by someone else. Reading helps us do that, if we approach it open to that possibility.

What should disappoint us the most as teachers is the student who reads only to confirm what he already thinks. That student is likely to become the adult who views only the television channels that tell him he is correct and has no more thinking to do. In the elementary schools, we don't often read about highly controversial topics and our youngest students probably don't regularly watch the news. We don't expect elementary school children to think through the complexities of difficult global social issues or to negotiate the political choices demanded by such events as elections. But we can nonetheless encourage them toward the approach to texts that will make them more responsive, responsible, and compassionate; we can recognize that they want to think about important issues that affect their neighborhoods and schools.

Perhaps, therefore, the most important thing we do with children is to ask them to consider how they might have revised their thinking as a result of reading. "How has this book or story touched you, made you think again about who you are or what you value? How has this text changed your thinking?" Such questions, in whatever form is most suitable for your students, may be the critical ones. These questions offer an invitation to make the reading meaningful for the reader. And that, after all, is what we should be seeking.

The World of Possible

Many years ago, Louise Rosenblatt said that she wrote *Literature as Exploration* as a "defense of democracy." By that she meant, we think, that readers who respected both the text and themselves were essential to preserve a democratic society. Our democracy, after all, is in some sense created and maintained in language. The Constitution, for instance, is expected to control and direct many of the nation's important decisions. We don't vest that power in an individual—a dictator or monarch—but rather we require an individual to swear that he or she will be bound by those words. Amending them, when it is found necessary to do so, is an arduous process, in part because as a society we respect those words and want them to govern and protect us.

But an educated citizenry, a populace who expects and demands clear and honest discourse, may be able to reject those who would use language to mislead, inflame, or enslave.

Words matter in a democracy, and thus it is vitally important that all members of the society respect them and attend closely to them. We will be in jeopardy if the leaders we select use words carelessly or deceitfully, if their words or if their statements are devoid of evidence or rationality. But an educated citizenry, a populace who expects and demands clear and honest discourse, may be able to reject those who would use language to mislead, inflame, or enslave.

Ultimately, we are teaching children to read the text of their own lives.

Protecting our democracy begins with a respect for the power of words. And where better to develop that respect than in a good book? If the thinking one does while reading that book disrupts complacency, if that thinking is responsive and responsible, if that thinking encourages compassion for others around us, both near and far, and a willingness to at least hear their stories or arguments, then we will be closer to creating the participants in our society that our democracy not only deserves but demands.

Ultimately, we are teaching children to read the text of their own lives. We want them open to possibility; open to ideas; open to new evidence that encourages a change of opinion. We want them using reading and writing as tools that help them in the re-vision of their own lives. We want them to have a better tomorrow. You are, for so many of these children, their best hope as schools stand as gatekeepers of a better tomorrow. As always, we are proud to stand beside you, though truly, as we have said before, we stand in awe of you. And we are excited to see what you do next.

Take Two: Conclusion
scholastic.com/
BeersandProbst

ACKNOWLEDGMENTS

WHEN WE BOTH BEGAN WRITING for teachers, we both wrote alone, as the single author of books or articles. It wasn't that we didn't want to collaborate; it was that we simply had never considered writing collaboratively. When we decided to write our first article together, we didn't know how to proceed. Would one of us write first and then the other edit? Would we divide the article into sections and each of us take certain parts and write those? Would we write bits at a time and swap the budding manuscript back and forth? We truly didn't know how to begin.

What we discovered during the writing of that first article is that our writing processes are about as different as writing processes can be. One of us likes to talk through the topic—over and over and over the other might say—until it feels right, until it has verbally taken a shape. The other of us likes to begin writing early—too early the other might say— letting the writing show us where we'll go. One of us is willing to say, "It's not right yet," again and again and again, one sentence at a time, while the other finds power in getting through bigger chunks before reflecting on revisions. One of us has the habit of starting the day with a phrase that the other at times hates, "So, last night, I was thinking. . . ." The other usually retorts, "Stop that damn thinking. No more thinking." But then, of course, we both stop to explore where new thoughts might take us.

We watch the work you do, we listen to your concerns, we hear your trials and tribulations, and all that affects us deeply.

And both of us discovered that we were going to have to figure out how to handle our differences, because if we were going to write collaboratively, we were going to actually have to collaborate. We weren't going to say, "You do this section and I'll do that one." That (for us) isn't collaboration; that was divide and conquer. We are more a "united we stand" team, we discovered.

So, we figured it out. We're still figuring it out. And in all that figuring out, we've discovered that we can't imagine writing without the other. More importantly, over the years, we've come to realize we can't imagine writing without you—classroom teachers, district supervisors, literacy coaches, administrators, and state leaders. Some of you directly affect our thinking by letting us into your classrooms, sharing your students' work with us, asking us questions, answering our questions, telling us what you're trying, trying what we think might help readers, and most important, telling us when what we have in mind is a bad idea (as many first ideas are). Others of you less directly, but no less importantly, help us by connecting with us via social media or through surveys we put into the field or during workshops. And many of you affect our thinking as we look in on what you are saying via your blog posts and social media. We watch the work you do, we listen to your concerns, we hear your trials and tribulations, and all that affects us deeply.

We must mention a few teachers and teacher leaders who have graciously and generously helped us think about issues in this book. Tara Smith, Allison Jackson, Jennifer Ochoa, Jeff Williams, and Paul Hankins directly affected—disrupted!—our thinking about ideas that were going into this book, and to them, we are immensely grateful.

The teachers of Solon City School District, Solon, Ohio, have always been willing to try our strategies and share their successes and concerns with us. The photos of children throughout these pages are from their classrooms. We are deeply grateful for their continued commitment to the work we share with them.

Special thanks to Eileen Ours, Linda Rief, Alison Aten Rash, Megan Clappin, and Heidi Weber for sharing their anchor charts and student work.

Additionally, colleagues Lester Laminack, Nancie Atwell, Penny Kittle, Linda Rief, Kelly Gallagher, Lucy Calkins, Teri Lesesne, Donalyn Miller, Sara Kajder, Ernest Morrell, Pam Allyn, Stephen Peters, Sara Holbrook, and Amelia Van Name Larson gave us much to consider and reconsider.

Trade book authors Chris Crutcher, Kwame Alexander, Laurie Halse Anderson, Sharon Draper, Andrew Smith, Jacqueline Woodson, and Sharon Creech showed us time and time again that the more important truths can be found in fiction and that the reader's job is to complete the journey the writer has begun.

All the thinking that went into writing this book would have remained merely ideas had Scholastic not stepped forward to both embrace the ideas for this book and to embrace us. Something happens when you walk into the Scholastic offices in New York City the first time. Is it the five-foot-tall Clifford waiting to say hello? Is it Harry Potter posed with his Quidditch broom? Perhaps it is the room filled with all the student writing from the Scholastic writing contests or the hallways decorated with winning student art. Maybe it's the credo for the company, written by founder M. R. R. Robinson, woven into the carpets. Or could it be the people throughout that building who come to work each day to bring book clubs and book fairs, trade books and magazines and professional books, into our nation's schools? Is it the magical combination of all those things? We aren't sure, but we have enjoyed our visits there and so appreciate the way we were welcomed by so many.

In particular, Lois Bridges, Goddess of All Things Possible (aka vice president and publisher of Scholastic Professional Books), believed in this book long before we knew the shape it would take. We appreciate the way she stayed calm when we kept changing the direction it would go. She learned quickly that a table of contents for us is merely a suggestion, a reason to have revision. As we learned more from you, we shifted— sometimes slightly and sometimes greatly—but Lois always held the course. We are grateful for her support. To think alongside Lois is to work with an editor who knows the field and is tireless in her support of improving literacy education for students.

But Lois would be the first to tell you that she doesn't work in isolation, and we came to agree that without the smart eye of Ray Coutu, editor-in-chief, this book would have not been what it is today. Ray's attention to detail, his understanding of where we were trying to go, and his ability to remember what we said one hundred pages ago so we wouldn't contradict ourselves on page one hundred and one was invaluable. Likewise, the smart thinking of Sarah Longhi, editorial director, helped us keep moving forward as she managed to watch all the details we would have overlooked. Special thanks to copy editor Danny Miller. If there are grammatical mistakes in this book, it's because we were too stubborn to take his advice.

We want to offer a special thank you to Brian LaRossa, art director. Working on a cover design and interior design of a book requires that the designer be part mind-reader and part creative genius. Brian embodies both. Each time we said, "No, this isn't quite it," but couldn't put into words what the "it" was, Brian defined what we could not articulate. As he handed the ideas to Maria Lilja, a member of his team, we saw seamless work between the two of them as images and words, as shape and content, merged into what you hold now.

But this book only matters if it gets into your hands, for it is your reading that makes these ideas real. So for us, having marketing people in the conversations is always important. From the beginning of the project, we appreciated the willingness of Scholastic Education's Linda Koons, senior vice president of publishing, and Pam Parker, marketing director, to read drafts of the manuscript and offer their insights on how to better our thoughts. The ideas in the book originated with us, but the ways of getting the book to you came from them.

If you've read our previous books, you know this is our first book with Scholastic. We trust the adage, "Make new friends/but keep the old./ One is silver/And the other gold." We believe we've not only extended our professional publishing circle, but have extended our circle of colleagues and people we now call friends. With that in mind, we must say thank you to two additional people at Scholastic who have generously and warmly welcomed us into the Scholastic family.

Greg Worrell, the president of Scholastic Education, cleared his packed calendar for us a number of times to talk through this project and others. We leave each meeting with Greg smarter and more hopeful for what we—this world of teachers—can indeed accomplish.

> You teach so much more than a standard; you teach students whom you claim as your own.

Dick Robinson, president and CEO of Scholastic, is someone we've long admired. To now sit in meetings with him, to hear him tell the story of how Scholastic came to be, to listen to him talk of why lifetime reading is so important, to watch him think through each idea, and to see him stand unwavering in his commitment to helping every child achieve his or her potential is to watch a literary giant in action. Dick offers all of us broad shoulders upon which to stand so we might each see further, and we are honored by his support.

While a publishing family is important, it's our own personal families we depend on most. They live their lives listening to us talk about you, about students, about policy issues, about school visits, about workshops and conferences, and about the funny things kids say. They listen to us read aloud paragraphs or sentences, they forgive us when in the midst of dinner-time conversations we rush to a piece of paper to jot down the idea we don't want to lose. They offer support that is constant, a support that allows us to do more than we thought we could.

And finally, we turn to you. For our youngest, you tie shoes, buy lunches, wipe tears, bend to the floor when your knees aren't sure they can make that trip back up once more. For our adolescents, you see apathy as insecurity and recognize that all too often anger is actually fear. You stay up late writing one more lesson, worrying about one more kid, reading one more chapter of one more professional book. You teach so much more than a standard; you teach students whom you claim as your own. You rise to the challenge, and for that, and so much more, thank you.

REFERENCES

Abodeeb-Gentile, Theresa, and Lisa Zawilinski. 2013. Reader Identity and the Common Core: Agency and Identity and Leveled Reading. *The Language and Literacy Spectrum*, 34–45.

Adams, Marilyn. 2006. The Promise of Automatic Speech Recognition for Fostering Literacy Growth in Children and Adults. In M.C. McKenna, L. D. Labbo, R.D. Kieffer, and D. Reinking (Eds.), *International Handbook of Literacy and Technology, Volume 2*. Mahwah, NJ: Lawrence Erlbaum Associates.

Allen, Linda K., Erica L. Snow, and Danielle S. McNamara. 2015. Are You Reading My Mind? Modeling Students' Reading Comprehension Skills with Natural Language Processing Techniques. Retrieved from Poughkeepsie, NY: Allington, Richard L. (2001). *What Really Matters for Struggling Readers: Designing Research-Based Programs*. New York: Addison-Wesley.

Allington, Richard L. 2012. *What Really Matters for Struggling Readers: Designing Research-Based Programs. (2nd Ed.)*. Boston, MA: Allyn-Bacon.

Allington, Richard and Anne McGill-Franzen. 2013. *Summer Reading: Closing the Rich/Poor Reading Achievement Gap*. New York: Teachers College Press.

Allyn, Pam and Ernest Morrell. 2016. *Every Child a Super Reader: 7 Strengths to Open a World of Possible*. New York: Scholastic.

Anderson, Richard C. 1984. Role of the Reader's Scheme in Comprehension, Learning, and Memory. In Richard C. Anderson, Jean Osborn, & Robert J. Tierney (Eds.), *Learning to Read in American Schools: Basal Readers and Content Texts* (pp. 197–308). Hillsdale, N.J.: L. Erlbaum Associates.

Anderson, Richard C., Jean Osborn and Robert J. Tierney. 1984. *Learning to Read in American Schools: Basal Readers and Content Texts*. Hillsdale, N.J.: L. Erlbaum Associates.

Anderson, Richard C. 1985. *Becoming a Nation of Readers: The Report of the Commission on Reading*. Washington, D.C.: National Academy of Education, National Institute of Education, Center for the Study of Reading.

Anderson, Richard C., Paul T. Wilson, and Linda G. Fielding. 1988. Growth in Reading and How Children Spend Their Time Outside of School. *Reading Research Quarterly, 23*, 285–303.

Argo, Jennifer J., J. Rui Zhu, and Darren W. Dahl. 2008. Fact or Fiction: An Investigation of Empathy Differences in Response to Emotional Melodramatic Entertainment. *Journal of Consumer Research* 34(5), 614–623.

Armbruster, Bonnie B. 2004. Considerate texts. In D. Lapp, J. Flood, & N. Farnan (Eds.), *Content Area Reading and Learning: Instructional Strategies* (2nd ed., pp. 47–58). Mahwah, NJ: Erlbaum.

Armbruster, Bonnie B. 1996. Considerate Texts. In Diane Lapp, James Flood, & Nancy Farnan (Eds.), *Content Area Reading and Learning: Instructional Strategies* (2nd ed., pp. 47–58). Boston: Allyn & Bacon.

Armbruster, Bonnie B., and Ian Wilkinson. 1991. Silent Reading, Oral Reading, and Learning from Text. *The Reading Teacher* 45(2), 154–155.

Atwell, Nancie. 1987, 1998, 2014. *In the Middle*. Portsmouth, NH: Heinemann.

Atwell, Nancie and Anne Atwell Merkel. 2016. *The Reading Zone, Second Edition*. New York: Scholastic.

Bal, P. Mattijs and Martijn Veltkamp. 2013. How Does Fiction Reading Influence Empathy? An Experimental Investigation on the Role of Emotional Transportation. Accessed at PLoS ONE 8(1): e55341. doi:10.1371/journal.pone.0055341 Bazerman, Charles. (1980). A Relationship between Reading and Writing: The Conversational Model. *College English, 41*(Six), 656–661.

Bazerman, Charles. 1980. A Relationship Between Reading and Writing: The Conversational Model. *College English 41*(6), 656–661.

Beach, Sarah Ann. 1993. Oral Reading Instruction: Retiring the Bird in the Round. *Reading Psychology, 14*, 333–338.

Beers, Kylene. 2003. *When Kids Can't Read, What Teachers Can Do: A Guide for Teachers*. Portsmouth, NH: Heinemann.

Beers, Kylene. 2009. The Sounds of Silence. *The Council Chronicle*, 14–16.

Beers, Kylene. 2009. The Genteel Unteaching of America's Poor. Urbana, IL: NCTE.

Beers, Kylene, and Robert E. Probst. 1998. Classroom Talk About Literature: The Social Dimensions of a Solitary Act. *Voices from the Middle* 16(2), 16–20.

Beers, Kylene, and Robert E. Probst. 2013. *Notice & Note: Strategies for Close Reading*. Portsmouth, NH: Heinemann.

Beers, Kylene, and Robert E. Probst. 2016. *Reading Nonfiction: Notice & Note Stances, Signposts, and Strategies*. Portsmouth, NH: Heinemann.

Beers, Kylene, Robert E. Probst, and Linda Rief (Eds.). 2007. *Adolescent Literacy: Turning Promise into Practice*. Portsmouth, New Hampshire: Heinemann.

Begum, Fateha Subhan. 2014. Changing Conceptions of Literacy and Identity in an Urban School. *Changing English: Studies in Culture and Education* 21(1), 14–23.

Bergmann, Jonathan, and Aaron Sams. 2012. *Flip Your Classroom: Reach Every Student in Every Class Every Day*. Eugene, OR: International Society for Technology in Education.

Blachowicz, Camille L. Z., and Donna Ogle. 2008. *Reading Comprehension: Strategies for Independent Learners* (2nd ed.). New York: Guilford Press.

Bloom, Paul. 2014, September 10, 2014. Forum: Against Empathy. Accessed at https://bostonreview.net/forum/paul-bloom-against-empathy.

Brodhead, Richard H., and John W. Rowe. 2015. *The Heart of the Matter: Around the Country*. American Academy of Arts & Sciences. Accessed at https://www.amacad.org/multimedia/pdfs/HeartOfTheMatter_AroundTheCountry.pdf.

Campione, Joseph C. 1981. *Learning, Academic Achievement, and Instruction*. Paper presented at the second annual conference on reading research of the study of reading, New Orleans, LA.

Carrubba, Christine. *Round Robin Reading: Is There Justification for Its Use or Are There Better Alternatives Available for Oral Reading Instruction?* College of William and Mary. Accessed at https://tvo.wikispaces.com/file/view/justify%20RRR.pdf.

Clay, Marie. 1975. *What Did I Write? Beginning Writing Behaviour*. Aukland, New Zealand: Heinemann.

Clay, Marie. 1982. *Observing Young Readers: Selected Papers*. Portsmouth, NH: Heinemann.

Coryell, Nancy G. 1927. *Contributions to Education: No. 275. An Evaluation of Extensive and Intensive Teaching of Literature: A Year's Experiment in the Eleventh Grade*. New York: Teachers College, Columbia University.

Cotton, Kathleen. 1988. *Instructional Reinforcement*. Portland, OR: Northwest Regional Educational Laboratory.

Cunningham, Anne E., and Keith E. Stanovich. 2003. Reading Matters: How Reading Engagement Influences Cognition. In James Flood, Julie M. Jensen, Dianne Lapp, & James R. Squire (Eds.), *Handbook of Research on Teaching the English Language Arts (2nd Edition)* (pp. 666–675). Mahwah New Jersey: Lawrence Erlbaum Associates.

Dewey, Caitlin. 2014. This is Not an Interview with Banksy. *The Washington Post*, October 22. Accessed at https://www.washingtonpost.com/news/the-intersect/wp/2014/10/21/this-is-not-an-interview-with-banksy/?tid=a_inl&utm_term=.b7fabb05bfe4.

Djikic, Maja, Keith Oatley, Sara Zoeterman, and Jordan B. Peterson. 2009. On Being Moved by Art: How Reading Fiction Transforms the Self. *Creativity Research Journal* 21(1), 24–29.

Early, Margaret. 1960. Stages of Growth in Literary Appreciation. *English Journal, 49*(3), 161–167.

Edwards Jr., Mark U. 1994. *Printing, Propaganda, and Martin Luther*. Berkeley: University of California Press.

EOA National Best Practices Center. 2016. Selecting Best Practices. Accessed at http://www.besteducationpractices.org.

Evans, M. D. R., Jonathan Kelley, Joanna Sikora, and Donald J. Treiman. 2010. Family Scholarly Culture and Educational Success: Books and Schooling in 27 Nations. *Research in Social Stratification and Mobility, 28*(2), 171–197.

Feitelson, Dina, and Zahava Goldstein. 1986. Patterns of Book Ownership and Reading to Young Children. *The Reading Teacher, 39*(4), 924–930.

Feuer, Alan, and Matthew Wolfe. 2014. A Tarantula Isn't Lost and Isn't Real. *The New York Times*, July 11. Accessed at https://www.nytimes.com/2014/07/12/nyregion/mexican-red-rump-tarantula-goes-missing-in-brooklyn-nyc-is-false.html.

Fisher, Douglas. 2004. Setting the Opportunity to Read Standard: Resuscitating the SSR Program in an Urban High School. *Journal of Adolescent & Adult Literacy 48*(2), 138–150.

Fives, Allyn, Dan Russell, Norean Kearns, Rena Lyons, Patricia Eaton, John Canavan, Carmel Devaney, and Aoife O'Brien, Aoife. 2014. The Association between Academic Self-Beliefs and Reading Achievement among Children at Risk of Reading Failure. *Journal of Research in Reading 37*(3), 215–232.

Fletcher, Jack M. 2006. Measuring Reading Comprehension. *Scientific Studies of Reading 10*(3), 323–330.

Fordham, Signithia, and John U. Ogbu. 1986. Black Students' School Success: Coping with the "Burden of 'Acting White.'" *The Urban Review, 18*(3), 176–206.

Fredrickson, Barbara L., Michael A. Cohn, Kimberly A. Coffe, Jocelyn Pek, and Sandra M. Finkel. 2008. Open Hearts Build Lives: Positive Emotions, Induced through Loving-Kindness Meditation, Build Consequential Personal Resources. *Journal of Personality and Social Psychology 95*(5), 1045–1062.

Gallagher, Kelly. 2004. *Deeper Reading: Comprehending Challenging Texts, 4–12*. Portland, Me.: Stenhouse Publishers.

Gallagher, Kelly. 2009. *Readicide: How Schools Are Killing Reading and What You Can Do About It*. Portland, Me.: Stenhouse Publishers.

Garan, Elaine M., and Glenn DeVoogd. 2008. The Benefits of Sustained Silent Reading: Scientific Research and Common Sense Converge. *The Reading Teacher 62*(4), 336–344.

Gee, James Paul. 1992. The Social Mind: Language Ideology and Social Practice. New York: Greenwood Publishing Group, Inc.

Goodman, Kenneth. 1982. Language and Literacy. Boston: Routledge & Kegan Paul.

Goodman, Kenneth, & Goodman, Yetta. 1983. Reading and Writing Relationships: Pragmatic Functions. Language Arts 60(5), 590–599.

Graves, Donald H. 1983. Writing: Teachers and Children at Work. Exeter, NH: Heinemann.

Green, Greg. 2012. My View: Flipped Classrooms Give Every Student a Chance to Succeed. Accessed at http://schoolsofthought.blogs.cnn.com/2012/01/18/my-view-flipped-classrooms-give-every-student-a-chance-to-succeed/.

Grenby, Matthew O. The Origins of Children's Literature. Accessed at https://www.bl.uk/romantics-and-victorians/articles/the-origins-of-childrens-literature.

Guthrie, John T., and Allen Wigfield. 2000. Engagement and Motivation in Reading. In M. L. Kamil, P. B. Mosenthal, P. D. Pearson, & Rebecca R. Barr (Eds.), *Handbook of Reading Research, Vol III* (pp. 403–422). Mahwah, NJ: Lawrence Erlbaum Associates.

Guthrie, John T., Susan Lutz, and Amy N. Ho. 2013. Modeling Relationships Among Reading Instruction, Motivation, Engagement, and Achievement for Adolescents. *Reading Research Quarterly, 48*, 9–26.

Hall, Leigh A. 2012. Rewriting Identities: Creating Spaces for Students and Teachers to Challenge the Norms of What It Means to Be a Reader in School. *Journal of Adolescent & Adult Literacy 55*(5), 368–373.

Hargreaves, Andy, and Michael Fullan. 2012. *Professional Capital: Transforming Teaching in Every School*. New York, NY: Teachers College Press.

Harper, Shaun R. 2010. An Anti-Deficit Achievement Framework for Research on Students of Color in STEM. *New Directions for Institutional Research, 2010*(148), 63–74.

Harste, Jerome C. 2009. Reading as identity. *Journal of Reading Education, 34*(3), 5–7.

Harste, Jerome, C., and Carolyn Burke. 1988. *Creating Classrooms for Authors*. Portsmouth, NH: Heinemann.

Harvey, Stephanie, and Anne Goudvis. 2000/2007. *Strategies that Work*. Portland, ME: Stenhouse.

Hass, Jim. 2016. For the Sake of Humanity, Teach the Humanities: Liberal Arts Education Is Essential to Good Citizenship. *Education Week*, November 14, 2016.

Head, Martha. H., and John E. Readance. 1992. Anticipation Guides: Enhancing Meaning through Prediction. In E. K. Dishner, T. W. Bean, E. Readence, & D. W. Moore. (Eds.), *Reading in the Content Areas: Improving Classroom Instruction* (third ed.). Dubuque, IA: Kendall/Hunt.

Heard, Georgia. 2016. *Heart Maps: Helping Students Create and Craft Authentic Writing*. Portsmouth, NH: Heinemann.

Herrman, John. 2016. Inside Facebook's (Totally Insane, Unintentionally Gigantic, Hyperpartisan) Political-Media Machine. *New York Times Magazine*, August 24, 2016. Accessed at http://www.nytimes.com/2016/08/28/magazine/inside-facebooks-totally-insane-unintentionally-gigantic-hyperpartisan-political-media-machine.html?_r=1

Heyns, Barbara. 1978. *Summer Learning and the Effects of Schooling*. New York: Academic Press.

Hiebert, Alfreda H., and Ray D. Reutzel. 2010. *New Directions for Teachers and Researchers* (Inc. TextProject Ed.). Newark, DE: International Reading Association.

Hoffman, Sandra J. 1982. *Preschool Reading Related Behaviors: A Parent Diary*. (Ph.D.), University of Pennsylvania, Dissertation abstracts International 43, 722A.

Huey, Edmund Burke. 1908. *The Psychology and Pedagogy of Reading, with a Review of the History of Reading and Writing and of Methods, Texts, and Hygiene in Reading*. New York,: Macmillan.

Ivey, Gay, and Karen Broaddus. 2001. "Just Plain Reading": A Survey of What Makes Students Want to Read in Middle School Classrooms. *Reading Research Quarterly 36*(4), 350–378.

Jesweak, Tonya Kay. 2015. Reader's Identity: How Identity and Literacy Can Work Together for Student Success in Middle School. Allendale, MI: Grand Valley State University. Accessed at http://scholarworks.gvsu.edu/coeawardhonor/7/.

Johnson, Dan R. 2012. Transportation into a Story Increases Empathy, Prosocial Behavior, and Perceptual Bias toward Fearful Expressions. *Personality and Individual Differences 52*(2), 150–155.

Jumpstart. (2009). *America's Early Childhood Literacy Gap*. Accessed at http://laup.net/images/stories/america s early childhood_literacy_gap.pdf

Kaestle, Carl F. 1988. The History of Literacy and the History of Readers. In Barry M. Kroll Eugene R. Kintgen, and Mike Rose (Ed.), *Perspectives on Literacy* (pp. 115). Carbondale, IL: Southern Illinois University Press.

Kamenetz, Anya. 2015. Several Florida School Districts Cut (Way) Back on Tests. NPRED: How Learning Happens. Accessed at http://www.npr.org/sections/ed/2015/04/29/402585146/several-florida-school-districts-cut-way-back-on-tests.

Katy News, The. 2015. Katy ISD Board Passes Resolution Calling for Elimination of High-Stakes State Testing. April 9. Accessed at http://thekatynews.com/?s=Katyisd+testing+resolution.

Keene, Ellin Oliver. 2012. *Talk About Understanding: Rethinking Classroom Talk to Enhance Comprehension*. Portsmouth, NH: Heinemann.

Kendeou, Pananyiota, and Paul van den Broek. 2007. Interactions between Prior Knowledge and Text Structure During the Comprehension of Scientific Texts. *Memory and Cognition 35*(7), 1567–1577.

Kidd, David Comer, and Emanuele Castano. 2013. Reading Literary Fiction Improves Theory of Mind. Accessed at http://www.sciencemag.org/content/early/recent / 3 October 2013 / Page 3 / 10.1126/science.1239918).

Kids and Family Reading Report, 5th edition. 2015. Accessed at http://www.scholastic.com/readingreport/.

Kim, James, and David M. Quinn. 2013. The Effects of Summer Reading on Low-Income Children's Literacy Achievement from Kindergarten to Grade 8: A Meta-Analysis of Classroom and Home Interventions, *Review of Educational Research 83*(4), 386–431.

Kittle, Penny. 2013. *Book Love: Developing Depth, Stamina, and Passion in Adolescent Readers.* Portsmouth, NH: Heinemann.

Kondo, Marie. 2014. *The Life-Changing Magic of Tidying Up.* New York: Ten Speed Press.

Koopman, Eva Maria (Emy), and Frank Hakemulder. 2015. Effects of Literature on Empathy and Self Reflection: A Theoretical-Empirical Framework. *Journal of Literary Theory 9*(1), 79–111.

Krashen, Stephen D. 1989. We Acquire Vocabulary and Spelling by Reading: Additional Evidence for the Input Hypothesis. *e73*: 440–64.

Kuhn, Melanie R. Dec. 2004/Jan. 2005. Helping Students Become Accurate Expressive Readers: Fluency Instruction for Small Groups. *The Reading Teacher 58*(4), 338–344.

Kuhn, Melanie R. (2016). What's Really Wrong with Round Robin Reading. *Ask a researcher.* Accessed at https://literacyworldwide.org/blog/literacy-daily/2014/05/07/what's-really-wrong-with-round-robin-reading-.

Laminack, Lester L. and Reba M. Wadsworth. 2012. *Bullying Hurts: Teaching Kindness Through Read Alouds and Guided Conversations.*

Langer, Judith A., and Sheila Flihan. 2000. Writing and Reading Relationships: Constructive Tasks. In Roselmina Indrisano & James R. Squire (Eds.), *Perspectives on Writing: Research/Theory/Practice.* Albany, New York: International Reading Association.

Lapp, Diane, and Douglas Fisher. 2009. It's All About the Book: Motivating Teens to Read. *Journal of Adolescent & Adult Literacy 52*(7), 556–561.

Lesesne, Teri S. 2003. *Making the Match: The Right Book for the Right Reader at the Right Time, Grades 4–12.* Portland, ME: Stenhouse Publishers.

Lyengar, S. 2007. To Read or Not to Read: a Question of National Consequence. Accessed at Washington DC: https://www.arts.gov/sites/default/files/ToRead.pdf.

Mar, Raymond A, Keith Oatley, and Jordan B. Peterson. 2009. Exploring the Link between Reading Fiction and Empathy: Ruling out Individual Differences and Examining Outcomes. *Communications 34*, 408.

McCombs, Jennifer Sloan, Catherine H. Augustine, Heather L. Schwartz, Susan J. Bodilly, Brian McInnis, Dahlia S. Lichter, Amanda Brown Cross. 2010. Making Summer Count: How Summer Programs Can Boost Children's Learning. Santa Monica, CA: Rand Corporation. Accessed at http://www.rand.org/content/dam/rand/pubs/monographs/2011/RAND_MG1120.pdf/.

McConn, Matthew. 2016. An Evaluation of Extensive and Intensive Teaching of Literature: One Teacher's Experiment in the 11th Grade. *Research in the Teaching of English 51* (2): 162–182.

McLean, Kate, Andrea V. Breen, and Marc Fournier. 2010. Constructing the Self in Early, Middle, and Late Adolescent Boys: Narrative Identity, Individuation, and Well-Being. *Journal of Research on Adolescence 20*(1), 166–187.

McNamara, Danielle S., and Walter Kintsch. 1996. Learning from Texts: Effect of Prior Knowledge and Text Coherence. *Discourse Processes 22*(3), 247–288.

McVee, Mary B., and Kailonnie Dunsmore, and James R. Gavelek. 2005. Schema Theory Revisited. *Review of Educational Research 75*, 531–566.

Meyer, B .J. F., & Rice, G. E. (1984). The structure of text. In P.D. Pearson, R. Barr, M.L. Kamil, & P. Mosenthal (Eds.), *Handbook of reading research* (pp. 319–351). New York: Longman.

Millward, Robert E. 1977. Round-Robin Is Not an Endangered Species. *Reading World 16*(4).

Moss, Barbara, and Terrell A. Young. 2010. *Creating Lifelong Readers through Independent Reading.* Newark, DE: International Reading Association.

Murray, Donald Morison. 1980. Writing Is Process: How Writing Finds Its Own Meaning. In T. R. Donovan & W. McClelland (Eds.), *Eight Approaches to the Teaching of Composition.* Urbana, IL: National council of teachers of English.

Nagy, William E., Richard C. Anderson, and Patricia A. Herman. 1987. Learning Word Meanings from Context During Normal Reading. *American Educational Research Journal*, 237–270.

Nation, Paul and James Cody. 2013. Vocabulary and Reading. In *Vocabulary and Language Teaching* edited by Ronald Carter and Michael McCarthy. Routledge Press, NY, NY. Pp. 97–111.

National Assessment Governing Board of the U.S. Dept. of Education. 2015. National Assessment of Educational Process, Reading. Washington, D.C.: Institute of Education Sciences. U.S. Dept. of Education.

National Endowment for the Arts. 2007. To Read or Not to Read: A Question of National Consequence. Accessed at Washington DC: https://www.arts.gov/sites/default/files/ToRead.pdf.

National Institute of Child Health and Human Development. 2000. Report of the National Panel Teaching Children to Read: An Evidence-Based Assessment of the Scientific Research Literature on Reading and Its Implications for Reading Instruction (NIH Publication No, 00-4769). Washington, DC: US Government Printing Office.

National Reading Panel. 2000. *Report of the National Reading Panel: Teaching Children to Read.* Washington, DC: National Institute of Child Health and Human Development.

Nell, Victor. 1988. *Lost in a Book: The Psychology of Reading for Pleasure.* New Haven, CT: Yale University Press.

Neumann, Susan B., and Naomia Moland. 2016. Book Deserts: The Consequences of Income Segregation on Children's Access to Print. *Urban education.* Accessed at http://uex.sagepub.com/content/early/2016/07/05/0042085 916654525. abstract.

Ogle, Donna. 1986. The K-W-L: A Teaching Model That Develops Active Reading of Expository Text. *The Reading Teacher 39*, 564–570.

Oliver, Mary. 1986. The Journey. In *Dream Work.* New York: The Atlantic Monthly Press.

Opitz, Michael F., and Timothy V. Rasinski. 1998. *Good-Bye Round Robin: 25 Effective Oral Reading Strategies.* Portsmouth, NH: Heinemann.

Ozuru, Yashuhiro, Kyle Dempsey, and Danielle S. McNamara. 2009. Prior Knowledge, Reading Skill, and Text Cohesion in the Comprehension of Science Texts. Learning and Instruction *Learning and Instruction 19*(3), 228–242.

Pearson, P. David, and Margaret Gallagher. 1983. *The Instruction of Reading Comprehension, Technical Report No. 297.* Retrieved from Urbana, IL: National Council Teachers of English.

Pearson, P. David, and Susie Goodin. 2010. Silent Reading Pedagogy: A Historical Perspective. In Alfreda H. Hiebert & D. Ray Reutzel (Eds.), *New Directions for Teachers and Researchers.* Newark, DE: International Reading Association.

Pearson, P. David, Jane Hansen, and Christine J. Gordon. 1979. The Effect of Background Knowledge on Young Children's Comprehension of Explicit and Implicit Information. *Journal of Reading Behavior 11*, 201–209.

Pew Research Center. May, 2016. News use across social media platforms, 2016. Retrieved from http://assets.pewresearch.org/wp-content/uploads/sites/13/2016/05/PJ_2016.05.26_social-media-and-news_FINAL-1.pdf.

Pink, Daniel, H. 2009. *Drive: The Surprising Truth About What Motivates Us.* New York: Riverhead.

Pressley, Michael. 2000. Comprehension strategies instruction. In J. Osborn & F. Lehr (Eds.), *Literacy for All: Issues in Teaching and Learning* (pp. 113–133). New York: Guilford.

Pressley, Michael, Wood, Eileen, Woloshyn, Vera E., Martin, Vicki, King, Alison, & Menke, Deborah. (1992). Encouraging Mindful Use of Prior Knowledge: Attempting to Construct Explanatory Answers Facilitates Learning. *Educational Psychologist, 27*(1), 91–109. doi:10.1207/s15326985ep2701_7

Probst, Robert E. 1992. Reader Response Theory and the Problem of Meaning. *Publishing Research Quarterly, 8*(1), 64–73. doi:10.1007/BF02680522

Probst, Robert E. 2001. Difficult Days, Difficult Texts. *Voices from the Middle, 9*(2), 50–53.

Public Schools of North Carolina. Retrieved 2016. Best Practices: A Resource for Teachers. Accessed at http://www.ncpublicschools.org/docs/curriculum/bpractices2.pdf.

RAND, Reading Study Group. 2002. *Reading for Understanding: Toward an R&D Program in Reading Comprehension*. Retrieved from Santa Monica, CA:

Raphael, Taffy, Becky W. Kirschner, and Carol Sue Englert. 1988. Expository Writing Program: Making Connections Between Reading and Writing. *The Reading Teacher*, 41(8), 790–795.

Rasinski, Timothy V., and James V. Hoffman. 2003. Oral Reading in the School Literacy Curriculum. *Reading Research Quarterly*, 38(4), 510–522. doi:10.1598/RRQ.38.4.5

Read, Charles, and Richard E. Hodges. 1982. Spelling. In *Encyclopedia of Educational Research*, 5th ed. edited by Harold Mitzel. New York: Macmillan, 1983.

Reutzel, D. Ray, Parker C. Fawson, and John A. Smith. 2008. Reconsidering Silent Sustained Reading: An Exploratory Study of Scaffolded Silent Reading. *The Journal of Educational Research* 102(1), 37–50.

Rief, Linda. 2014. *Read Write Think*. Portsmouth, NH: Heinemann.

Riswanto, Risnawati, and Detti Lismayanti. 2014. The Effect of Using KWL (Know, Want, Learned) Strategy on EFL Students' Reading Comprehension Achievement. *International Journal of Humanities and Social Science* 4(7)(1), 225–233.

Rosenblatt, Louise. M. 1938/1995. *Literature as Exploration* (first and fifth eds.). New York: Modern Language Association.

Rubin, Jared. 2008. Printing and Protestan=ts: An Empirical Test of the Role of Printing in the Reformation. *Review of Economics and Statistics* 96(2), 270–286.

Seidman, Dov. 2007. *HOW: Why HOW We Do Anything Means Everything*. Hoboken, NJ: John Wiley.

Shanahan, Timothy. 2006. Does he really think kids shouldn't read? *Reading Today*, 23(6), 12.

Silverman, Craig. 2016. This Analysis Shows How Fake News Stories Outperformed Real News on Facebook. *BuzzFeedNews*, November 16. Accessed at https://www.buzzfeed.com/craigsilverman/viral-fake-election-news-outperformed-real-news-on-facebook?utm_term=.qtgr6004j#.pd52Dyyng

Smagorinsky, Peter. 2001. If Meaning is Constructed, What Is It Made From? Toward a Cultural Theory of Reading. *Review of Educational Research* 71, 133–169.

Snyder, Lynn. 2010. Reading Expository Material: Are We Asking the Right Questions? *Topics in Language Disorders* 30(One), 39–47. doi:10.1097/TLD.0b013e3181d098b3

Taba, Hilda. 1967. *Teacher's Handbook for Elementary Social Studies*. Reading, MA: Addison-Wesley.

Tatum, Alfred W. 2009. *Reading for Their Life*. Portsmouth, NH: Heinemann.

Tatum, Alfred W. 1999. Reading and African American Male: Identity, Equity, and Power. *Journal of Adolescent & Adult Literacy* 43(1), 62–64.

Thinking About the Reading/Writing Connection with P. David Pearson. March-April 2002. Retrieved from http://www.nwp.org/cs/public/download/nwp_file/1330/Thinking_About_the_Reading_and_Writing_Connection.pdf?x-r=pcfile_dhttp://www.nwp.org/cs/public/download/nwp_file/1330/Thinking_About_the_Reading_and_Writing_Connection.pdf?x-r=pcfile_d

Thompson, Gail L., Susan Warren, and LaMesha Carter. 2004. It's Not My Fault: Predicting High School Teachers Who Blame Parents and Students for Students' Low Achievement. *The High School Journal*, 87(3).

Trudel, Heidi. 2007. Making Data-Driven Decisions: Silent Reading. *Reading Teacher* 61(4), 308–315.

Tuck, Kathy D., and Dwight R. Holmes. 2016. *Library/Media Centers in US Public Schools: Growth Staffing and Resources* (executive summary). Accessed at https://www.nea.org/assets/docs/Trends%20in%20School%20Library%20Media%20Centers%20Executive%20Summary.pdf

Wagner, Tony and Ted Dintersmith. 2015. *Most Likely to Succeed: Preparing Our Kids for the Innovation Era*. NYC: Scribner.

Wilhelm, Jeffrey D. and Michael W. Smith. 2014. *Reading Unbound: Why Kids Need to Read What They Want—and Why We Should Let Them*. New York: Scholastic.

Wolf, Maryanne. 2007. *Proust and the Squid: The Story and Science of the Reading Brain* (1st ed.). New York, NY: HarperCollins.

Wong, Alia. 2016. Where Books Are All But Nonexistent. *The Atlantic*. Accessed at http://www.theatlantic.com/education/archive/2016/07/where-books-are-nonexistent/491282/.

Worthy, Jo, and Nancy Roser. 2010. Productive Sustained Reading in a Bilingual Class. In *Revisiting Silent Reading: New Directions for Teachers and Researchers*, ed. Elfrieda Hiebert, and D. Ray Reutzel. Newark, DE: International Reading Association.

Trade Books Cited

Applegate, Katherine. *The One and Only Ivan*

Basher, Simon. *Basher Science: Climate Change*

Beals, Melba Pattillo. *Warriors Don't Cry: A Searing Memoir of the Battle to Integrate Little Rock's Central High*

Cherry, Lynn and Gary Braasch. *How We Know What We Know about Changing Climate*

Collins, Suzanne. *The Hunger Games*

Conrad, Joseph. *Heart of Darkness*

Curtis, Christopher Paul. *The Watsons Go to Birmingham–1963*

David, Laurie and Gordon Cambria. *The Down to Earth Guide to Global Warming*

de la Peña, Matt. *Last Stop on Market Street*

Dickens, Charles. *A Tale of Two Cities*

Draper, Sharon M. *Stella by Starlight*

Erickson, John R. *Hank the Cowdog*

Freeman, Don. *Corduroy*

Garcia-Williams, Rita. *One Crazy Summer*

Haddix, Margaret Peterson. *Among the Hidden*

Hanlon, Abby. *Dory Fantasamagory*

Hawthorne, Nathaniel. *The Scarlet Letter*

Henkes, Kevin. *Chrysanthemum*

Holm, Jennifer and Matthew Holm. *Baby Mouse*

Howe, Deborah and James Howe. *Bunnicula: A Rabbit-Tale of Mystery*

Hopkinson, Deborah. *Up Before Daybreak*

Kurlansky, Mark. *World Without Fish*

Lantier-Sampon, Patricia. *Rachel Carson: Fighting Pesticides and Other Chemical Pollutants*

Levine, Ellen. *Henry's Freedom Box: A True Story from the Underground Railroad*

Lobel, Arnold. *Frog and Toad*

Lord, Cynthia. *A Handful of Stars*

Lowry, Lois. *The Giver*

Marshall, James. *George and Martha*

Mobin-Uddin, Asma. *My Name Is Bilal*

Mochizuki, Ken. *Baseball Saved Us*

Naylor, Phyllis Reynolds. *Shiloh*

Novak, B. J. *The Book with No Pictures*

Patterson, Katherine. *Bridge to Terabithia*

Paulsen, Gary. *Hatchet*

Polacco, Patricia. *Bully*

Ryan, Pam M. 2002. *Esperanza Rising*. New York: Scholastic.

Schmidt, Gary. *The Wednesday Wars*

Scieszka, Jon. *The True Story of the Three Little Pigs*

Simon, Seymour. *Global Warming*

Soto, Gary. *Too Many Tamales*

Taylor, Mildred D. *Roll of Thunder, Hear My Cry*

Tonatiuh, Duncan. *Separate Is Never Equal: Sylvia Mendez and Her Family's Fight for Desegregation*

Waller, Robert James. *Bridges of Madison County*

Woodson, Jacqueline. *Brown Girl Dreaming*

Woodward, John. *DK Eyewitness Climate Change*

Articles for Children Cited

"Are Trampolines Dangerous?" *Storyworks*. September 2016. Pp. 26–27.

"China's Left-Behind Children." *Junior Scholastic*. September 5, 2016.

"Doctor Says It's Best to Keep Volume at Medium or Lower with Ear Buds." *The Washington Post*, November 11, 2016. Adapted by Newsela staff. Accessed at https://newsela.com/articles/headphone-earbuds/id/24095/.

"Garana's Story: A Day in the Life of a Young Afghan Refugee." *National Geographic Explorer*. Originally published September 1, 2002.

"Growing Up Muslim in Post 9/11." *Scholastic Scope*. September 2016.

INDEX

ABOUT THE AUTHORS

Kylene Beers, author of *When Kids Can't Read/ What Teachers Can Do* (Heinemann, 2003) and **Robert E. Probst,** author of *Response and Analysis, 2nd edition* (Heinemann, 2002), are respected authorities on reading instruction. Kylene—focusing more on reading strategies—and Bob—focusing more on engagement and literary analysis—present together to show teachers and administrators how coordinated attention to strategies and engagement help readers, especially those who struggle, improve.

Kylene, a former middle school teacher, and Bob, a former high school teacher, have both taught at the university level. Now a Senior Reading Advisor to Secondary Schools at Teachers College Reading and Writing Project, Kylene was the 2008–2009 President of the National Council of Teachers of English. Bob, now Professor Emeritus of English Education at Georgia State University, is co-author, with Kylene, of *Notice and Note: Strategies for Close Reading* (Heinemann, 2012); *Reading Nonfiction: Stances, Signposts, and Strategies* (Heinemann, 2015); and *Disrupting Thinking: Why How We Read Matters* (Scholastic, 2017). They are co-editors, with Linda Rief, of *Adolescent Literacy: Turning Promise into Practice* (Heinemann, 2007).

Kylene has taught in public schools and held positions at the University of Houston and the Comer School Development Program at Yale University. She has served as editor of the NCTE journal *Voices from the Middle* and is a contributor to national literacy journals. Bob also taught in public schools before becoming a district supervisor of language arts. He has served as a board member for both the NCTE Commission on Reading and the Conference on English Education (of NCTE) and as a column editor for *Voices for the Middle*. They are both recent recipients of the Conference on English Leadership Outstanding Leader Award, and both have served as the senior authors of the literature textbook *Elements of Literature*.

Bob and Kylene are nationally and internationally known consultants who speak and write about issues of literacy. You can follow both on Twitter: @KyleneBeers and @BobProbst.